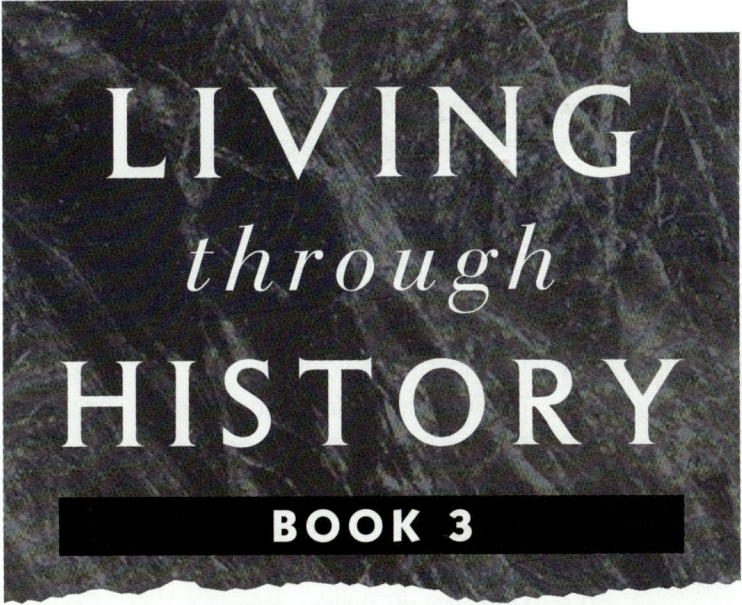

Britain 1750 – 1900
and
The Twentieth Century World

Fiona Reynoldson
and
David Taylor

CONTENTS

Britain 1750–1900

Chapter 1
- Britain 1750–1900: an introduction — 4
- **1.1** Britain gains an empire — 8
- **1.2** The slave trade — 12
- **1.3** The Black Hole of Calcutta — 18
- **1.4** Keeping in touch — 20
- **1.5** Get thee to Australia — 22
- **1.6** The Irish Famine 1845–8: the problem — 26
- **1.7** The Irish Famine 1845–8: solutions? — 28

Chapter 2
- **2.1** The Industrial Revolution — 30
- **2.2** The Agricultural Revolution — 32
- **2.3** Thomas Turner: village shopkeeper — 34
- **2.4** Steam: all change? — 36
- **2.5** Living and working conditions in Industrial Britain — 38
- **2.6** Maria Woolf: cholera victim — 46
- **2.7** Bradford woolcombers: dangerous and deadly work — 48
- **2.8** Titus Salt: a caring mill owner — 50
- **2.9** Saltaire: a gentle prison? — 52
- **2.10** Samuel Greg: a risk taker? — 54
- **2.11** Esther Price: a runaway apprentice — 56
- **2.12** Down the pit — 58
- **2.13** Getting about — 62
- **2.14** Living in Industrial Britain — 68

Chapter 3
- **3.1** Wars, riots and rebellions — 72
- **3.2** The American Revolution — 74
- **3.3** The gift of liberty — 78
- **3.4** The French Revolution — 80
- **3.5** Napoleon – Emperor of France — 84
- **3.6** The British Protest: Ned Ludd and Captain Swing — 88
- **3.7** The British Protest: Rebecca — 90
- **3.8** The British Protest: the Chartists — 92
- **3.9** Martha Carpenter: a country childhood — 94
- **3.10** Martha Carpenter: grown-up in London — 96

Twentieth Century World

Chapter 1		The Modern World: an introduction	98
	1.1	The First World War 1914–18	102
	1.2	The First World War: the trenches	104
	1.3	Cowards and traitors?	108
	1.4	The suffragettes go to war	112
	1.5	The Treaty of Versailles	118
Chapter 2	2.1	The rise of the dictators	120
	2.2	The Second World War	128
	2.3	The battle for Britain	132
	2.4	Bombs, bombs, bombs	134
	2.5	Keeping the children safe?	136
	2.6	Winnie's war	138
	2.7	The secret armies: the resistance movements in occupied Europe	140
	2.8	The secret armies: the Special Operations Executive	142
	2.9	Collaborators and traitors	144
	2.10	Secrets and spies	146
	2.11	The GIs: a different kind of invasion	148
	2.12	Germany – a divided nation	150
	2.13	The Japanese Empire – a short-lived success	152
	2.14	The Holocaust	156
Chapter 3	3.1	The Cold War	162
	3.2	The Cuban missile crisis	164
	3.3	Europeans go home	166
	3.4	The war in Vietnam	170
	3.5	The United Nations: an organisation for peace?	174
	3.6	The United Nations: an organisation for war?	176
	3.7	Postwar Britain: early childhood memories 1947–52	178
	3.8	Postwar Britain: schoolgirl memories 1952 onwards	180
	3.9	South Africa – a united nation?	182
	Glossary		188
	Index		190

BRITAIN 1750–1900: AN INTRODUCTION

All change

There were many changes in Britain between 1750 and 1900. This book is about these changes and what they meant for people who lived at the time.

Changes at work

In 1750 most people lived in small villages in the countryside. They farmed the land for a living. There was not very much industry. The main industry was making woollen cloth. This was done in people's homes on small hand-worked machines.

By 1900 this had changed. Now most people lived in big towns. They worked in factories which had steam-driven machines. Huge amounts of goods were sold to other countries. Ports, such as London, Liverpool and Bristol, grew at this time.

Changes in transport

In 1750 transport was poor. The roads were bad. People walked or travelled on horseback. Goods went by river or horse-drawn wagons.

By 1900 the roads were much better. Canals had been built and there were railways and steamships. Good transport was needed to take goods to market.

LONDON BEFORE 1850

Source A

Source B

Even London could seem peaceful in the early 1800s. Source A shows St Martin's Lane in 1825. It is not very busy. The church is called St Martin's-in-the-Fields. Source B shows people buying milk fresh from the cow in St James' Park in the middle of London.

In 1750 most people lived in villages and made cloth in their own homes.

In 1900 most people lived in towns and worked in factories.

Questions

1 Read page 4. Copy and complete these sentences.

In 1750 most people lived in _____. They _____ the land. By 1900 most people lived in _____. They worked in _____. Transport was better. There were roads, _____, _____ and _____.

2 What can you learn about Britain in the period 1750–1900 from **Sources A–D**?

LONDON IN ABOUT 1900

By 1900 people bought their milk from dairies (shops that sold milk, cream and butter) or carts that went from door to door. Source C shows Mr Morrison's dairy in London in 1905. Source D shows Trafalgar Square and the church of St Martin's-in-the-Fields in 1902.

Source C

Source D

The British Empire

Between 1750 and 1900 Britain built up a huge empire. An empire is when one country takes over and rules a lot of other countries. Britain grew rich selling goods to the Empire (see pages 8–9). It also got cheap raw materials and food from the Empire.

Emigration

Between 1750 and 1900 about 14 million people emigrated (left Britain) to other countries. They went to make a fresh start in life. Many went to America. Others went to live in countries that were part of the Empire, such as Australia and New Zealand.

A growing population

The number of people living in Britain rose quickly between 1750 and 1900. In 1750 there were about 7 million people. This had risen to 37 million by 1900. This was partly because people were healthier and living longer (see diagram).

Source E

1750   1900

Population
7 million | 37 million

People living in towns
13% | 87%

Life expectancy
1750: Men 31, Women 33
1900: Men 45, Women 48

Deaths at birth
1750: Babies lived / Babies died at birth
1900: Babies died at birth / Babies lived

Britain, 1750 and 1900.

The Salvation Army helped poor people a lot. Here two midwives are visiting a mother.

Source F

Wars

Other countries also had empires. This sometimes led to war. For example, Britain and France went to war over land in America and India (1756–63).

What about the workers?

Between 1750 and 1900 working people started to fight for their rights. They were badly paid and could not vote. They wanted a better life. They were encouraged by the French Revolution of 1789. This was when the poor people of France rioted and threw out the king.

British workers formed trade unions to get better wages. By 1900 most men could vote and life was better. Women could not vote until 1918!

The British navy beat the French navy in the Battle of Trafalgar (1805). Britain needed a strong navy to defend the Empire.

Questions

1 Read **Emigration**.
   a What is emigration?
   b How many people emigrated between 1750 and 1900?
   c Why did they emigrate?
   d Where did they go to?

2 Look at the diagram on page 6. Write a paragraph saying what it shows.

1.1 BRITAIN GAINS AN EMPIRE

A huge empire

An empire is formed when one country takes over and rules many other countries. The countries that are ruled over are called colonies.

In 1750 Britain did not have many colonies. Politicians said they would be too costly to run. But they changed their minds.

By 1900 Britain had built up a huge empire which covered one-quarter of the world.

Queen Victoria was the head of all this land and one of her titles was 'Empress'.

Britain builds an empire

1 Trade. Some people said Britain would get rich by trading with the Empire.

British merchants could export (sell) their goods to the colonies and import (buy) goods cheaply, such as cotton and sugar.

2 Progress. Some people said other countries would **benefit** from being under British control. They would learn about science and machines and become Christians.

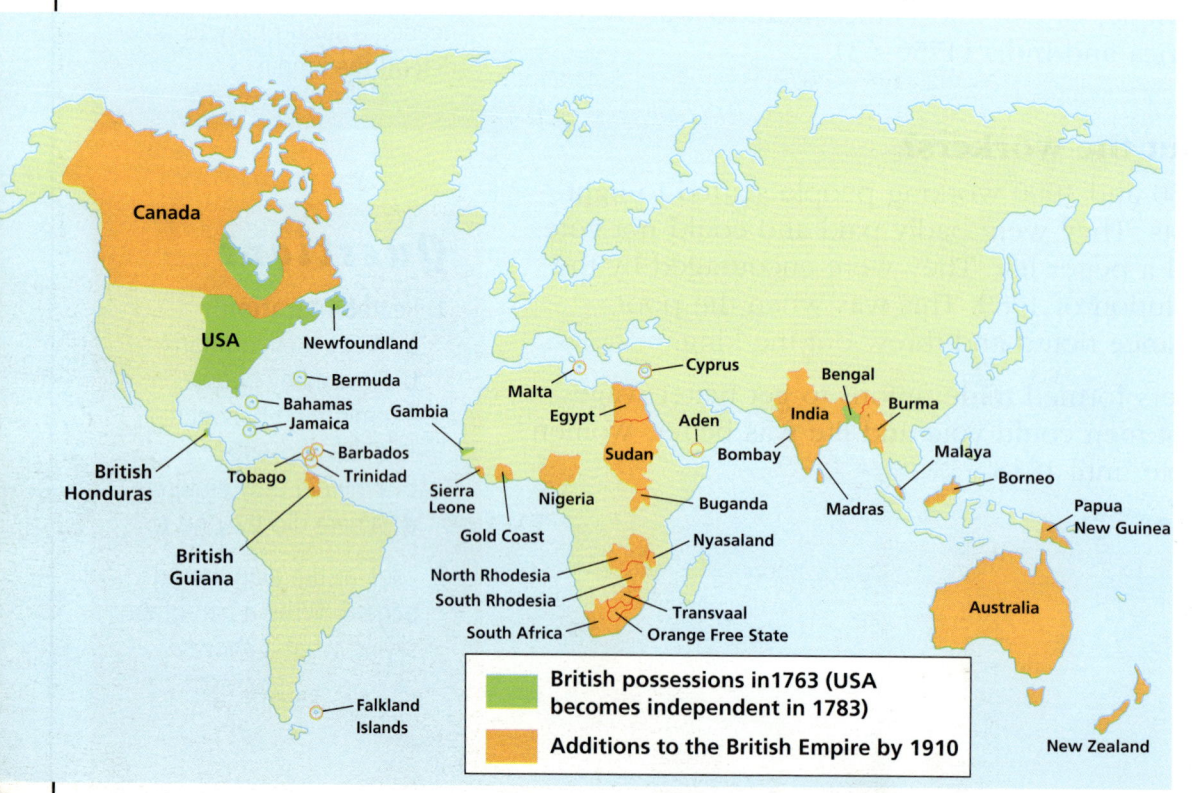

The British Empire in 1763 and 1910.

Queen Victoria presenting a bible to a foreign prince.

How the Empire was built up

1 Prizes. Britain sometimes acquired land or territory as a prize for winning wars.

Canada and India were taken in 1763 after a war against France.

Ceylon (now known as Sri Lanka) and parts of Southern Africa were gained in 1815 after Britain had beaten Napoleon, the French Emperor.

Hong Kong was taken in 1842 after a war with China.

A stuffed elephant on display at the Great Exhibition of London in 1851. The exhibition showed the world how strong British industry was. There were over 13,000 things on display.

2 Wars of conquest. Sometimes Britain went to war with the aim of taking over other countries. Parts of South Africa and Egypt were won like this (see Sources C and D).

3 By agreement. Some land was taken by making an agreement with another country. Singapore, for example, agreed to let the British build a naval base there in 1819.

4 By exploration. Some land was discovered by explorers. Captain James Cook discovered Australia and New Zealand in 1770. He claimed them for Britain.

Emigration

During the 1800s, over ten million people emigrated from Britain to live in different parts of the British Empire. All sorts of people went. Many wanted to make a 'new start' in life.

Trade and the British Empire

1 Strict rules. Britain made up some strict rules about trade which the colonies had to keep to. These rules helped Britain more than they did the colonies. Here are some examples.

- The colonies could only trade with Britain.
- The colonies had to use British ships to carry their goods.
- Taxes were put on goods made in the colonies, making them dearer than British goods.

Source D

A British soldier tells how he escaped from the Zulus at the Battle of Isandhlwana in 1879.

Huge numbers of Zulus came over the hills. There must have been about 20,000 of them.

They came right up to our camp. Nearly all of the Zulus had guns. Bullets were flying everywhere.

Many British soldiers were killed.

I reached safety by charging through the thinnest part of the Zulus' line.

Source C

A painting of the Battle of Isandhlwana in South Africa in 1879. The Zulus of South Africa beat the British in this battle. William Gladstone, a British politician, said that the Zulus were only fighting to defend their homes and that they did not have any guns.

2 Cheap raw materials. Britain was able to buy cheap cotton, sugar, cocoa and tea from the colonies.

They were made into products in British factories and sold in Britain and other countries. The British factory owners and merchants made big profits.

3 Cheap food. When large steamships came into use in the mid-1800s Britain was able to buy cheap food from the colonies.

Wheat came from Canada and meat and butter from Australia and New Zealand.

4 Big ports. Trading with the colonies meant that bigger ports had to be built.

London, Liverpool and Bristol all grew bigger to cope with the increase in trade.

The slave trade

Britain also made a lot of money from the slave trade. You can read about this terrible trade in human beings on pages 12–17.

Questions

1 Read **A huge empire** on page 8.
   a What is an empire?   b What are colonies?

2 Read **Britain builds an empire** on page 8. Why did Britain build up an empire?

3 Read **How the Empire was built up** on page 9.
   a Make a list of some of the countries in the British Empire.
   b Find as many of them as you can on the map on page 8.

4 Read **Trade and the British Empire** on pages 10 and 11. Copy and complete these sentences.
Britain got cheap _____ and _____ from the colonies. The large amount of trade meant that ports such as _____ , _____ and _____ grew in size.

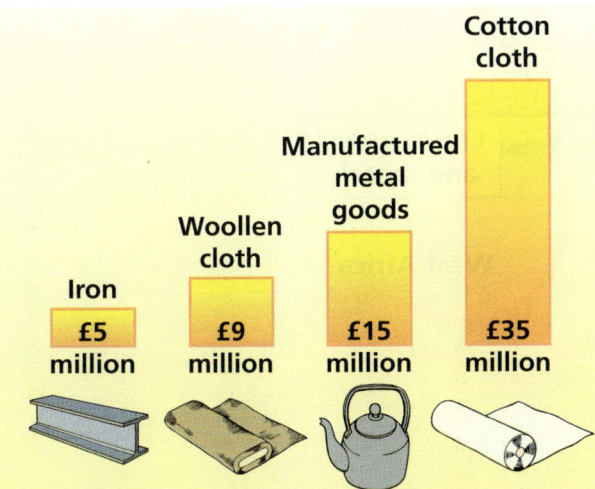

Money Britain earned from exports in 1850.

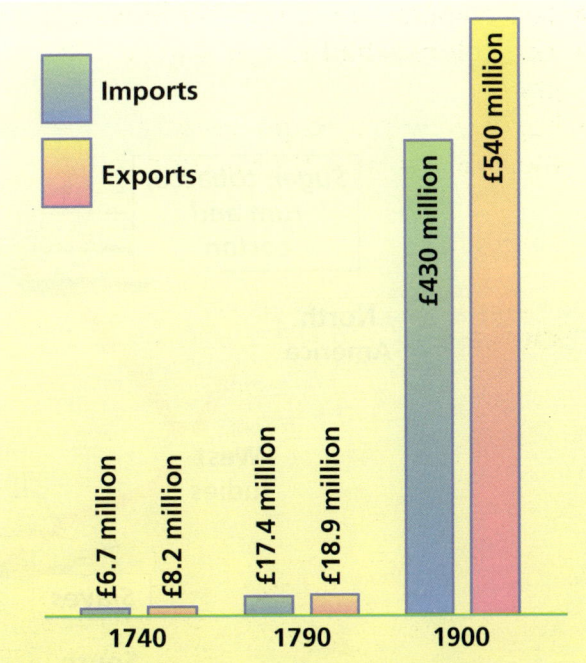

British imports and exports, 1740–1900.

1.2 THE SLAVE TRADE

How did the slave trade work?

There were three journeys involved in the slave trade, which is why it was also called the triangular trade (see the map below).

Journey 1: Ships went from Britain to West Africa loaded with pots, pans, kettles, cloth and guns. These goods were exchanged for black slaves.

Journey 2: The ships then sailed across the Atlantic Ocean to the West Indies or America. This was known as the middle passage. It was a horrific journey for the slaves. The slaves were packed tightly into the ships and there was hardly any room to move. The sea was often very rough.

When they landed, the slaves were sold to work on plantations (large farms which grew sugar, cotton or tobacco).

Journey 3: The ships then sailed back to Britain loaded with sugar, tobacco, rum and cotton.

Source A

This is what two ships' captains said about the slave trade.

- The slaves have about as much room as a man in a coffin. It is almost impossible for the slaves to move.
- I never want to see such things again. Trading slaves is dreadful.

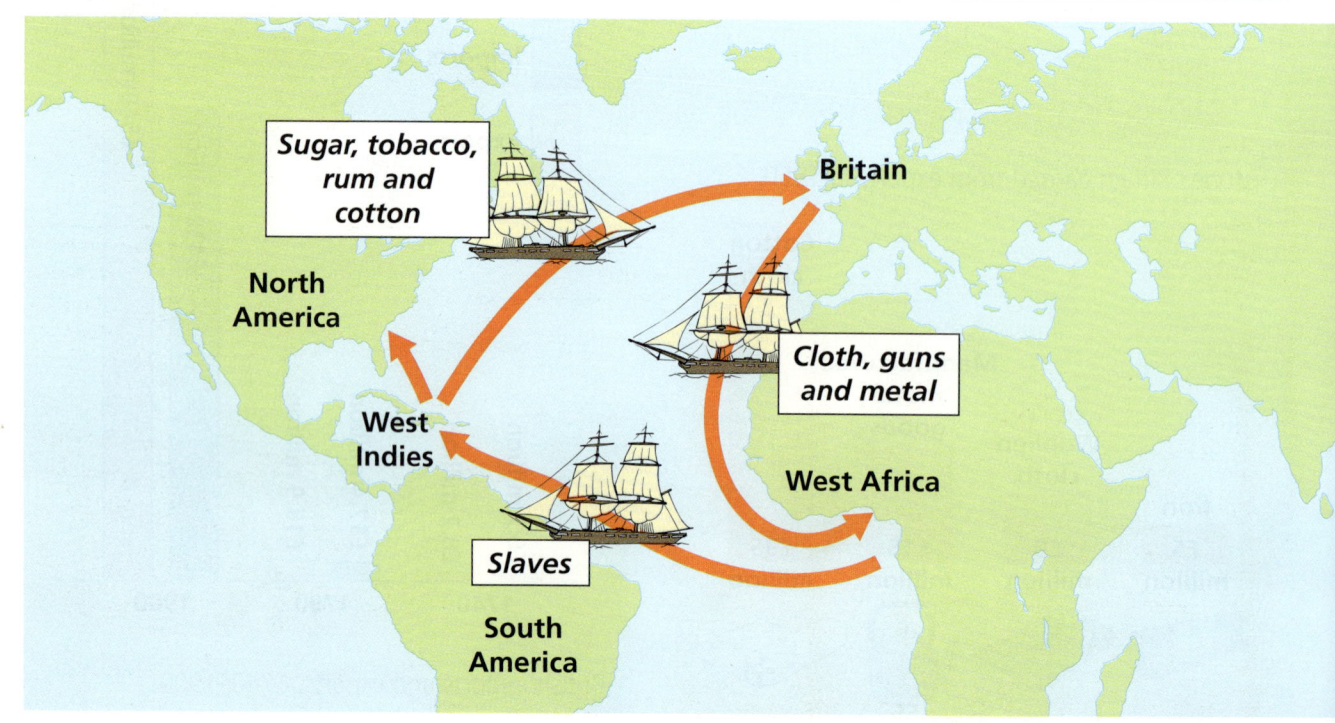

This map shows the three journeys of the triangular trade.

How Britain gained from the slave trade

People in Britain could buy cotton, tobacco and sugar cheaply

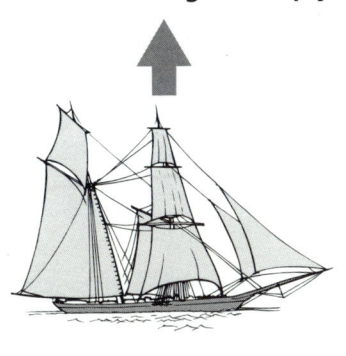

British merchants grew rich. They built factories, canals and railways with the money they made

Slavery in Britain

Many black slaves were brought to Britain from America and the West Indies.

They were bought by rich people to work as servants. It was the fashion to have a black servant in your house.

At first, people thought the slave trade was a good thing. But when they found out how cruel it was, some people changed their minds. (Look at the cartoon.)

Questions

1. Look at the map on page 12. What was traded on each journey of the triangle?
2. Read page 13. How did Britain gain from the slave trade?
3. Read **Slavery in Britain**.
   a. Why did rich people in Britain have black servants?
   b. Why did people start to think the slave trade was bad?

1750 — "It's silly to say the slave trade is wrong. They have a better life as slaves, not savages." / "Besides, we don't encourage it, do we? Pour more tea James!"

1790 — "Have you read Equiano's story of being a slave? And heard Mr Granville Sharp?" / "It's just one slave's bad experience. As for Granville Sharp, I'm told he's been misled."

1791 — "Where's James?" / "I gave him his freedom. Granville Sharp has shown he was right. I've read these leaflets that show slavery is wrong. Pour more tea Betty!"

1795 — "Are you going to the abolitionist meeting this afternoon?" / "Of course! Everyone with any sense knows slavery is wrong – have you seen the latest newspaper article?"

Changing attitudes to slavery.

Plantation owners

The plantation owners bought slaves and made them work very hard. When the crops were sold, the plantation owners made a big profit.

Plantation owners lived in grand houses.

Abolitionists

Some people in Britain began to say the slave trade was cruel and should be banned. They were called **abolitionists**. Two of them were Thomas Clarkson and William Wilberforce.

The plantation owners said that if they did not use slaves then cotton, tobacco and sugar would be dearer in Britain.

Source B

Source C

From a modern school history book.

In the 1700s Bristol slave ships made a profit of £8,000 every trip. Liverpool had over 100 slave ships. Together the two ports brought in £1,000,000 per year from slavery.

Source D

Said by a Liverpool man in 1795.

Slave ships have all sorts of people on board – lawyers, drapers, tailors, barbers and grocers. They all hope to make money out of the trip.

Trading ports

Liverpool, Hull, Bristol and Lancaster were the ports which made the most money from the slave trade. They grew into important cities.

Dodshon Foster, a Lancaster merchant, made money from the slave trade. Many people thought there was nothing wrong with trading in slaves.

THE LONG FAMILY

The Long family owned sugar plantations on the West Indian island of Jamaica.

1 **Samuel Long** set up a sugar plantation in Jamaica in 1655. He left £12,000 when he died in 1683 – a great deal of money at the time.

2 **Charles Long** went to live in England in 1700. He ignored his plantation in Jamaica. In 1707 a friend in Jamaica wrote to Charles saying that the slaves were hungry and the buildings were falling down. Charles took no notice. He was making enough money from the plantation anyway!

3 **Edward Long** became a plantation owner in 1757. He married Thomas Beckford's daughter. (Beckford was the richest plantation owner in Jamaica.) In 1769 Long became ill and retired to England.

Edward Long thought slavery was a good thing. He wrote books saying why the slave trade should be kept. Long thought that black people were not as good as white people.

He said:
Black people smell and do not know the difference between right and wrong. They are cruel to their children.

Source E

A picture of a mill used to crush the juice out of sugar cane.

The slaves are too well-dressed and too clean for it to be a true picture of what life as a slave was really like.

Questions

1 Read **Source C** on page 14. How much money did slave ships make?

2 Read **Abolitionists** on page 14.
   a What did they say about the slave trade?
   b What did the plantation owners say?

3 Would you trust **Souce E** as evidence about slavery? Explain your answer.

Black people in Britain

Many black people came to live in Britain.

Some came with plantation owners who were returning to live in Britain. Some came as sailors and servants. But many arrived as slaves.

You can read about what happened to some of them on these pages.

FRANCIS BARBER

Francis Barber was born a slave in Jamaica.

In 1750 he was brought to Britain by Captain Bathurst. He worked as a servant in Captain Bathurst's house. Francis was taught to read and write. When Captain Bathurst died in 1752, Francis went to work for Dr Johnson. Francis was allowed to get married in 1776.

When Dr Johnson died in 1782, he left all his property to Francis.

Francis then set up a school in Staffordshire. He died in 1801.

Runaways

Some slaves ran away from their masters. The masters placed adverts in newspapers to try and find them:

Hannah Press, a maid, ran away on 2 March. She has brownish skin and is of middle height. She was wearing a light gown and a petticoat and speaks in a broad Yorkshire accent.

She took with her a tankard, a plate, and six knives and forks, all made of silver.

John Bowman ran away from his master last Monday. He is 19 years of age, 5' 3" tall and has brown skin.

He has a sullen look and was wearing a wig and a blue coat.

Laws which freed slaves in the British Empire

1807: Trading in slaves was banned.
1833: Slaves in the British Empire were set free.

Source F

It was the fashion for rich people to have black servants in the 1700s.

JAMES SOMERSET

James Somerset, a black slave, was brought to Britain in 1769.

In 1771 he ran away but was recaptured by his master, Charles Stewart.

Stewart handed James to the captain of a ship.

He told the captain to take James to Jamaica and sell him.

Granville Sharp wanted the slave trade stopped.

He heard about James Somerset and took the case to court.

The judge was Lord Mansfield. He said that James could not be taken to Jamaica and was to be freed.

Lord Mansfield made a speech saying,

Slavery is hateful. It is wrong and should not be allowed. The black man must be freed.

James was set free but no one knows what happened to him.

Fears and rumours.

Questions

1 Read **James Somerset**.
   a Who was James Somerset and what happened to him?
   b Who took the case to court?
   c What did the judge say?

2 Read page 16.
   What happened in 1807 and 1833?

1.3 THE BLACK HOLE OF CALCUTTA

The East India Company
In 1600 a group of British merchants set up the East India Company. Merchants in the company traded with India. They brought cotton cloth, spices and dyes back to Britain. They made a big profit from selling these goods in Britain. Some of the profits were given to the government.

War with France
The French also had a trading company in India. In 1756 Britain and France went to war over land in India and America.

In India, the French asked the ruler of Bengal to attack the British base at Calcutta. There are two different stories about what happened next!

The British side of the story
The British say that the ruler of Bengal captured Calcutta. He threw 146 British soldiers into a tiny prison. It was cramped and stuffy.

The next morning 123 prisoners were dead. The prison was so tiny that they had suffocated. The British called the prison the 'Black Hole of Calcutta'. The story was told in British history books for many years afterwards.

The Indian side of the story
Indian historians say that no such event happened. They say that the British made the event up, because they wanted people to think that the Indians were cruel.

Some interesting facts

- No mention of the Black Hole was ever made to the East India Company.

- Britain and India made a peace treaty in 1757. The Indians said they would pay money to British people who had been attacked. But no mention was made of the Black Hole.

- An Indian history book was written a few years after. It lists attacks on the British by the Indians. There is no mention of the Black Hole.

A cartoon of the Black Hole from a British school history book.

Source A

THE BLACK HOLE OF CALCUTTA
Shut all night in a tiny room, without water, all but 23 of the 146 Britons died.

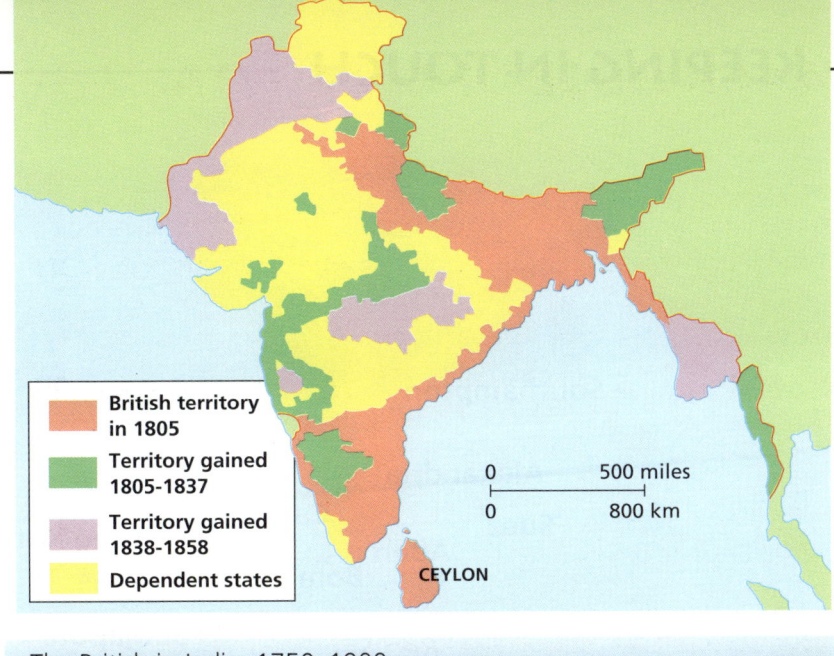

The British in India, 1750–1900.

ROBERT CLIVE

1743: Clive went to live in India. He was important in the East India Company.

1757: He won the Battle of Plassey against the Indians.

1764: Clive was made the Governor of Bengal. He became very rich. People wondered where he had got his money from.

1773: Clive fell ill and returned to Britain. He was taken to court and accused of stealing government money. He was found not guilty.

1774: He committed suicide.

The Battle of Plassey, 1757

On 23 June 1757 Robert Clive attacked the ruler of Bengal at Plassey. The British bribed the soldiers in the Bengali army to change sides.

The battle which followed only lasted a few hours. The British won. The ruler of Bengal was later found dead in a river.

Britain takes control of India

By 1763 the French had been driven out of India. After this the British took control of the country.

In 1877 Queen Victoria was made the Empress of India.

India was so important to Britain that it was called the 'jewel in the crown' of the Empire.

India wins its independence, 1947

During the 1920s and 1930s Mahatma Gandhi said India should be free of Britain. In 1947 India was given its independence. It could now run its own affairs.

Questions

1 Read **The British side of the story**.
   What do the British say happened in Calcutta in 1756?

2 Read **The Indian side of the story**.
   What do the Indians say happened?

3 Read **Some interesting facts** and **Source A** on page 18.
   Which of the two stories about the Black Hole of Calcutta do you think is more likely to be true? Why?

1.4 KEEPING IN TOUCH

Writing letters

The British Empire stretched to all parts of the world. The only way for people to keep in touch with family and friends was by writing letters.

Steamships

From the 1850s steamships were the quickest form of transport.

The Peninsular and Oriental Steam Navigation Company (P&O for short) had a fleet of steamships. They carried letters, soldiers and **cargo** from Britain to all parts of the Empire.

The electric telegraph

The electric telegraph was invented in 1838. It enabled messages to be sent along wire cables, which were laid on the seabed. In 1866 an electric cable was laid under the Atlantic Ocean and by 1870 a cable had been laid between Britain and India.

Overland route between Alexandria and Suez (before the Suez Canal was opened in 1869).

The places where Frank Kendall worked for P & O.

The *Great Eastern* steam ship, which laid the first telegraph cable under the Atlantic.

Questions

1. Look at the map and read **Extract 1**.
   Write down Frank's route from Southampton to Bombay in 1858.

2. Read **Extract 2** and **Extract 3**.
   What did Frank say about:
   a Life in Bombay
   b Life in Australia?

Source A

FRANK KENDALL (1839–1907)

Frank Kendall worked for P&O. His work took him all over the world.

Frank kept a diary of what happened to him. These extracts are from his diary.

Extract 1
1858: Southampton to Bombay

17 February: Reached Gibraltar in five days. There are 250 soldiers on board. The ship has been rolling about in the rough seas.

28 February: Arrived at Alexandria. We went across land to Suez by railway and donkey.

9 March: We arrived at Aden and heard that the Ava had sunk on its way to Calcutta. It was worth £70,000. P&O will have to pay for the mail which was lost.

18 March: Arrived at Bombay. I started work straight away in the P&O offices. It is very busy!

Extract 2
1858: Working in Bombay

20 March: There are three British people and twelve Indians working in the office.

People say that it will not be long before a telegraph cable is laid from India to Britain. Then we shall be able to speak to Britain in a matter of hours.

23 March: I am sharing a house with three others. My servant does not speak any English. They tell me he is a good worker.

19 June: The drainage in Bombay is terrible. When it rains the streets get flooded. They are like sewers. Many people fall ill with cholera and fever. Everything gets mouldy and damp.

Extract 3
1859: Suez and Australia

In 1859 P&O sent Frank to Suez and then to Australia. He went on the journey to learn about life on board a P&O ship.

28 March: Arrived at Suez. Some other passengers are changing to our ship. They are moaning because there is some missing luggage.

We left for Aden. A man was spotted in the sea about three miles away. He had fallen overboard but by the time the ship's lifeboat got there he had probably been eaten by sharks.

21 April: At Aden. We have taken 240 tons of coal on board. It is all over the decks. We need a lot of coal because the next bit of the journey is very long.

14 May: In Australia. Sydney Harbour is beautiful. Both Sydney and Melbourne have fine shops and markets. Things are cheaper here than in Bombay. Australia is very lively. I would love to live here.

12 July: The telegraph is now laid to Aden.

Kendall went back to Bombay on 10 September 1859. He went back to Melbourne in 1865. He stayed in Melbourne until he retired.

1.5 GET THEE TO AUSTRALIA

Transportation

The government wanted to get rid of criminals. So it sent them abroad to the colonies. This was called **transportation**.

At first, criminals were sent to America. Then America became independent in 1783. It refused to take criminals from Britain. So the criminals were sent to Australia instead.

The first fleet, 1787

The first fleet of ships, carrying 759 convicts, left Portsmouth for Australia in May 1787. Captain Arthur Phillip was in charge. The fleet arrived at Botany Bay in Australia in January 1788.

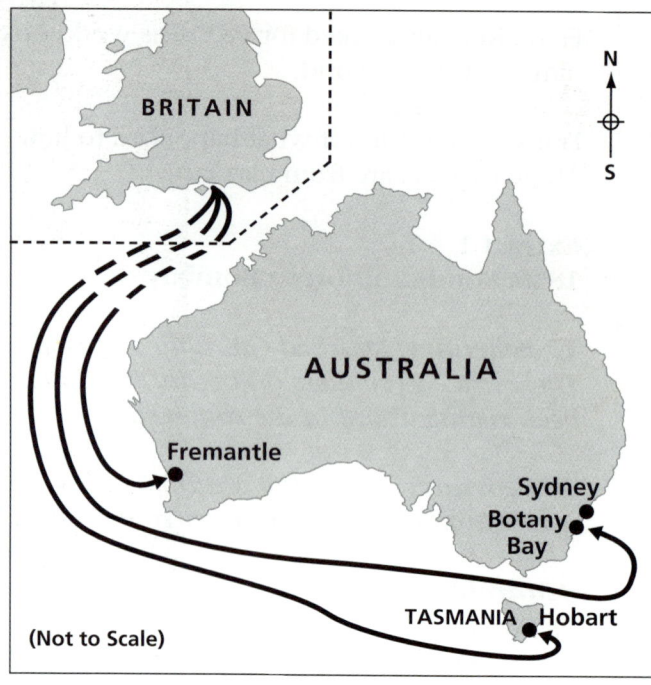

Source A

Punishments at Gloucester Law Courts, 1826.

William James — For breaking into a house and stealing cheese.

Transportation for 7 years.

Thomas James — For breaking into a house and stealing shirts.

Death by hanging.

George Cooke — For breaking into a house and stealing a blanket.

Transportation for 7 years.

Richard Mee — For stealing a bottle of brandy.

Transportation for 7 years.

Elizabeth Jones — For stealing cloth and other crimes.

Transportation for 7 years.

Captain Phillip was going to build a settlement at Botany Bay. But the land was sandy and swampy. So he built a settlement further up the coast instead. He called it Sydney, after the British Colonial Secretary, Lord Sydney.

Between 1788 and 1867, over 150,000 convicts were transported to Australia.

Who was transported?

Transportation was used as a punishment for all sorts of crimes.

1 Murderers were sometimes transported, rather than being hanged.

2 Petty criminals were often transported for things such as stealing cheese and handkerchiefs.

3 In 1830 over 500 farm labourers were transported for smashing threshing machines.

4 In 1834 six men from Tolpuddle in Dorset were transported for setting up a trade union. They became known as the Tolpuddle Martyrs (see pages 24–5).

Questions

1 Read **Transportation**. What was transportation?

2 Where were convicts sent after 1783?

3 Read **Who was transported?**
   a What sort of crimes were people transported for?
   b Does it surprise you that some people were transported for small crimes? Explain your answer.

4 Read **Source C**. How was James Pollock treated in Tasmania?

Source B

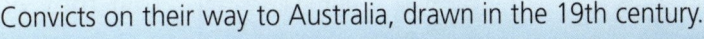

Convicts on their way to Australia, drawn in the 19th century.

Source C

James Pollock was transported to Tasmania. His master was very cruel. This is how he was treated.

My master was so cruel I ran way. I was on the run for four days. I was captured by a policeman and taken to court. My master told the court that I was lazy. He said that he treated me well.

I was given fifty lashes of a whip and sent back to my master. He was even more cruel. I had to carry logs on my back. It was such hard work I ran away four more times!

Each time I was caught and given fifty lashes. My back was in a real mess.

Harsh treatment

The convicts were often treated badly on the way to Australia. They were usually chained up and flogged (beaten) for doing next to nothing. Many died on the journey.

When the ships arrived in Australia, the convicts were made to clear bushland and build roads and farms.

Most of the convicts were treated like slaves (see Source C). Only a lucky few worked for a kind master.

The Tolpuddle Martyrs

George Loveless, James Brine, Thomas Standfield, John Standfield, James Loveless. The other 'martyr' was James Hammett.

A harsh punishment?

In 1834 six men from Tolpuddle in Dorset were transported to Australia for seven years. What had they done to get this harsh punishment? Read on.

Life in Tolpuddle

Most men in Tolpuddle were farm labourers. Life was very hard for them.

They lived in small, damp cottages. The wages were only about 50 pence a week.

A trade union

The workers in Tolpuddle told the farmers that they could not make ends meet.

They asked for a small rise in wages. But, instead, the farmers said they were going to cut the wages to 30 pence a week.

The farm workers, led by George Loveless, decided to form a **trade union**.

They hoped this would help them to get a decent wage. The men who joined the union took an **oath of loyalty** to the union.

The magistrates clamp down

The farmers and local magistrates were worried. They were scared that the workers would get too powerful and there would be a revolution.

The farm workers had not broken the law by forming a trade union.

But it was against the law to swear an oath of loyalty. The magistrates put a notice up saying so (see Source D).

Source D

This notice was put up in Tolpuddle warning people about taking illegal oaths.

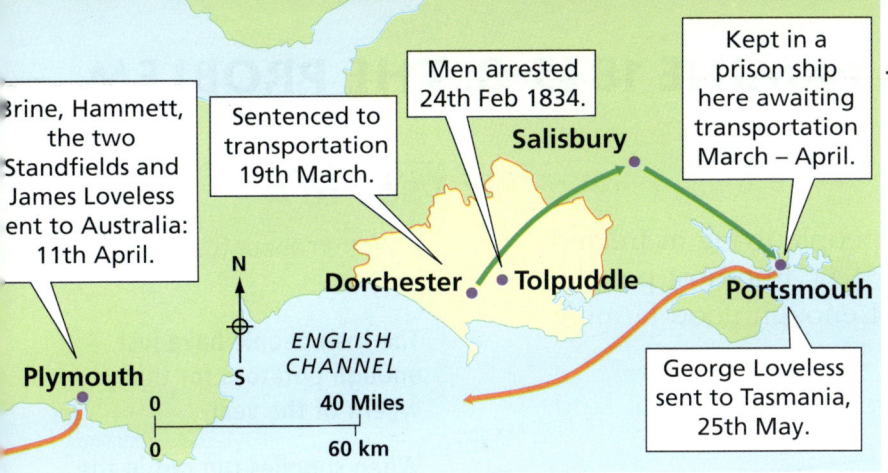

The arrest and transportation of the Tolpuddle Martyrs.

Source E

These words were spoken by George Loveless in court.

My lord, if we have broken the law, we have not done it on purpose. We have not hurt anyone.

We only wanted to protect our families from hunger.

Arrest

On 24 February 1834 George Loveless and five other men were arrested (see box on page 24). They were taken to court in Dorchester, found guilty and sentenced to seven years' transportation. It was a very cruel punishment. It was done to frighten other workers from joining trade unions.

To Australia

On 27 March 1834, five of the men were taken to a prison ship in Portsmouth. George Loveless was too ill to travel.

On 11 April 1834, the five men left Plymouth bound for Australia.

They arrived in Australia on 17 August 1834. They were kept in a prison camp and then sent to work on farms. They were treated like slaves.

George Loveless left Portsmouth for Tasmania on 25 May 1834.

Anger and a pardon

People in Britain were angry with the government. They thought the Tolpuddle men had been badly treated. People went on marches calling for them to be brought home.

In March 1836 the government gave the six men a free pardon. Only James Hammett came back to Tolpuddle to live. The other five men went to live in Canada in 1844.

Martyrs

The six men became heroes and have gone down in history as the Tolpuddle Martyrs.

Questions

1 Read **Life in Tolpuddle**. What was life like for farm workers in Tolpuddle?

2 Read **A trade union**. Why did some of the workers start a trade union?

3 Read **The magistrates clamp down** and **Arrest**. Why were the six men transported to Australia?

4 Read **Anger and a pardon**. Why do you think the six men were given a pardon in 1836?

25

1.6 THE IRISH FAMINE 1845-8: THE PROBLEM

Population and the land

In 1821 there were 6.8 million people living in Ireland. This went up to 8.2 million by 1842. But most people were farmers and there was not enough good farming land to go round.

Most Irish farmers only had a very small piece of land, which was wet and soggy.

Potatoes the main food

The Irish people lived mainly on potatoes. They were easy to cook and could also be fed to the animals. But what would happen if the potato crop failed?

Blighted potatoes

In 1845 the potatoes caught **blight**, a disease which made them black and slimy. The potatoes stank. They were unfit to eat.

This was serious. If it happened again, millions of people would face famine and starvation.

Source A

Written about the Irish in 1844.

The Irish people have just enough potatoes for thirty weeks of the year.

When supplies run out in the spring they will have no food until the new potatoes are ready in the summer.

People are forced to beg for food at this time.

Source B

How the Irish lived before the Famine.

Blight again

The winter of 1846 was very wet. Once again the potatoes had blight. Field after field was full of rotting potatoes. The smell was terrible. It was a disaster.

Millions of Irish people were left without food. Famine and starvation had arrived.

Disease follows

About 100,000 people died from hunger. A further 900,000 caught dreadful diseases. Hungry people have no strength to fight off germs. People died from:

- Flu and measles.
- Scurvy, a disease which made teeth drop out and legs turn black.
- Typhus, which caused a rash, fever and a swollen black face.

Source C

Said by a visitor to an Irish village in 1846.

I went into some of the poor cottages. What I saw was horrible. In one cottage I found six starving people. They looked like skeletons and were huddled on some filthy straw. They all had a fever and were moaning.

A funeral during the Irish potato famine.

Source D

Questions

1. Read **Population and the land**.
   a How much did the population of Ireland go up?
   b What did this mean for most people?

2. Read **Blighted potatoes**.
   What is blight?

3. Read **Blight again**.
   Why was 1846 a disaster for the Irish people?

4. Read **Disease follows**.
   a How many people died of hunger?
   b How many people died from disease?
   c Why did disease spread so quickly?
   d What were the killer diseases?

5. Read **Source C**.
   The visitor to this cottage was shocked by what he saw. Explain why.

1.7 THE IRISH FAMINE 1845–8: SOLUTIONS?

The starving Irish people needed help. What was done to help them?

1 Relief Committees set up

Rich people set up committees to provide shelter and food. They did their best, but too many people were starving for them all to be helped.

2 Maize brought from America

Ireland was governed by Britain at this time. Robert Peel, the Prime Minister, ordered maize (corn on the cob) to be brought from America.

But the Irish people did not like maize. They made it into a sort of porridge and called it Peel's **Brimstone**. They had no choice but to eat it.

3 Jobs building roads

The government built lots of new roads. The idea was to give people jobs. Then they would have some money to buy food.

But Ireland did not need the roads, so it was a waste of time. The government should have improved the land so that crops other than potatoes could be grown. But the government did not want to give money directly to landowners. The government did not think it was right for it to give money directly to people.

4 Workhouses given extra money

Many people went to the local workhouse hoping to get some food (see Source B).

The government gave the workhouses extra money and supplies of maize to help them cope. But it was too little, too late.

5 Fares paid to emigrate

A lot of people were so poor, they could not pay the rent. The landlords decided to **evict** them. Families were thrown out of their houses and turned out on to the streets. It was very cruel.

Many evicted people left Ireland for ever. They emigrated to America and Canada to start a new life. Their fares were paid by the local relief committees. It was cheaper than having to feed and shelter them.

Great suffering

The famine caused great suffering. By 1851 one million people had died of hunger and disease. Another million left Ireland to live in another country.

Source A

This was said by William Bennett, an Englishman. He went to Ireland with clothes and turnip seeds to give away. Here he is talking about the soup kitchens which were set up in some towns. They served a porridge made from maize.

Every day about 800 families are given some porridge to eat. This has helped the poor people a lot.

Source B

A crowd of starving people waiting outside a workhouse, in the hope of being fed.

Source C

Sir William Butler, an Irish soldier, describes an eviction he had seen as a boy.

One day I watched some families being evicted (thrown out) from their homes.

The poor people were dragged out into the road by the sheriff's men. Their houses were pulled down. The roofs were burned down and the walls battered in by crowbars.

I was twelve at the time. But if someone had handed me a gun, I would have shot the sheriff's men.

Questions

1 Read page 28.
   a List five kinds of help given to the Irish people.
   b Write two or three sentences about each one.

2 Read **Source C**.
   a What was it like to be evicted?
   b Would you trust what Sir William Butler says? Explain your answer.

3 Read page 28 again.
   Do you think enough was done to help the Irish? Explain your answer.

2.1 THE INDUSTRIAL REVOLUTION

Britain in 1750

In 1750 there were only seven million people living in Britain. Most people lived in small villages in the countryside. The only really big town was London.

Farming was the most important job. There were no factories. Some people made woollen cloth in their own homes to earn some extra money. This was called the domestic system.

Britain changes

Britain changed in the next hundred years. By 1850 most people lived in towns and worked in factories. We call this change the Industrial Revolution.

What happened to change Britain?

1. In the 1780s a steam engine was invented which could turn machinery. Steam power was quick and reliable. Soon there were lots of factories. They had steam-powered machinery that could make lots of goods. Most of the factories were in the north of England, where there was plenty of coal for the steam engines.

2. More factories meant more coal had to be mined to drive the steam engines. More iron was needed to build the machines.

Source A

A steam engine built in 1788. Steam engines were very powerful. One steam engine could turn several machines.

Source B

A coal mine in County Durham, 1844.

Source C

An engraving of a textile mill in Derby.

3 The factories needed workers. So large towns grew up next to the factories.

4 People moved into the towns from the countryside. They could no longer grow their own food. Farming had to improve so that more food could be grown to feed the townspeople.

5 Better transport was needed to take goods to market. Roads were improved and canals and railways were built.

By 1850 Britain made more goods than any other country. It was the 'workshop of the world'.

Questions

1 Read **Britain in 1750**.
   a What did most people do for a job?
   b Where did most people live?
   c What was the domestic system?

2 Read **Britain changes**.
   a Where did most people live in 1850?
   b Where did most people work in 1850?
   c What do we call this change?

3 What other changes took place in Britain at this time?

Source D

The world's first iron bridge, over the river Severn in Shropshire. It was built in 1781 by Abraham Darby. This painting was done in 1788.

2.2 THE AGRICULTURAL REVOLUTION

Strip farming

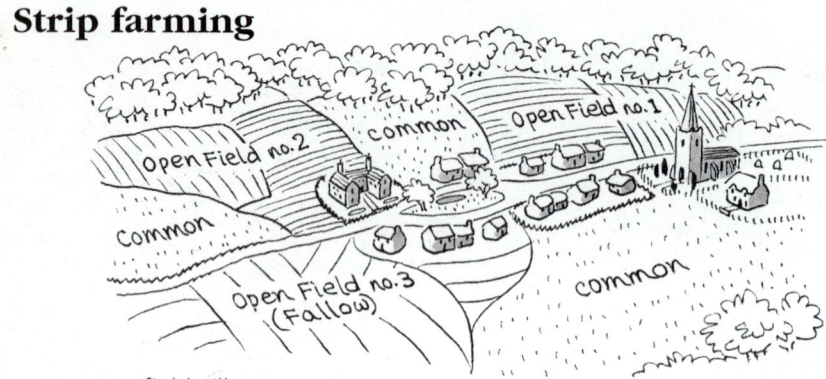

An open field village.

In the early 1700s most people lived in villages and worked on the land. Most villages had three large open fields, which were divided into strips.

Every farmer had strips in each of the fields. They had to walk across the village from strip to strip. This wasted a lot of time.

Each year one of the fields was left **fallow** (empty). Nothing was grown on it, so that the soil could recover. This was a waste of land. The villagers grazed their cattle and sheep on the common land.

> **The Norfolk Rotation System** ▶
> Each crop takes different nutrients from the soil, so they can be grown one after the other each year. Livestock can be put in the field of clover. As they eat, they also manure the fields.

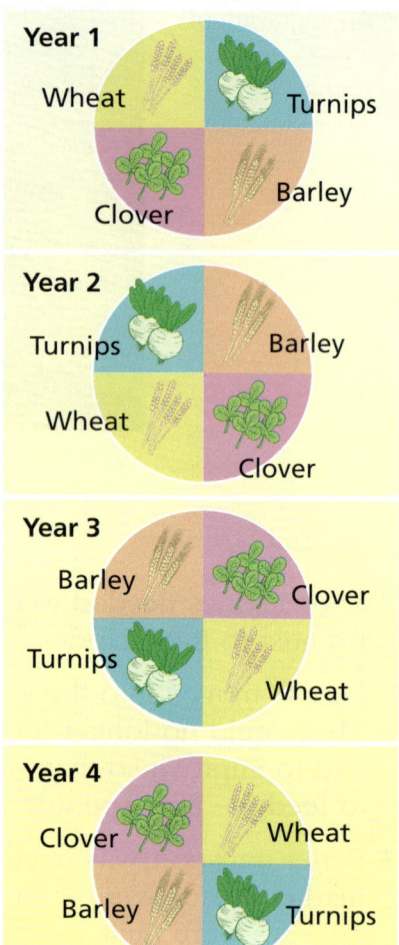

Source A

The Haymakers painted by George Stubbs in 1786

Source B

From a government report written in 1842.

Most cottages are made of mud with piles of filth near to the door.

The people who live in these cottages are poor. They dress in rags and live on bread and potatoes.

Enclosures

After 1750 the population of Britain rose. More food had to be grown. A better way of farming was needed. So villages were **enclosed**.

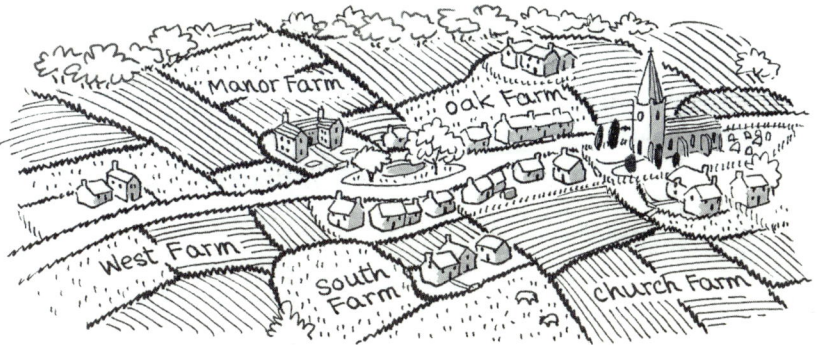

An enclosed village.

The strips were done away with. Now farmers had their land all together. It was fenced or hedged off from their neighbour. The common land was also turned into enclosed fields. This hit the poor people hard. They now had nowhere to graze their animals.

Improved farming methods

Enclosed fields led to better ways of farming. Seed drills and threshing machines came into use. There was no need to leave land empty each year (see diagram on page 32). Much more food was produced. Fatter animals were also produced. Farmers began to make big profits. But the new machinery meant that fewer workers were needed. Many lost their jobs.

Bad times

After 1870 cheap meat and wheat came into Britain from New Zealand and America. British farming then went through a bad period.

Questions

1. Read **Strip farming**. Why was strip farming wasteful?

2. Read **Enclosures**.
   a. Why was a better way of farming needed after 1750?
   b. How did enclosures change a village?

3. Read **Improved farming methods**. What new methods now came into use?

4. Read **Bad times**. Why did British farming have a bad time after 1870?

1710		1795
370 lb	Cattle	800 lb
70 lb	Calves	140 lb
28 lb	Sheep	80 lb
18 lb	Lambs	50 lb

The average weight of livestock in 1710 and 1795.

2.3 THOMAS TURNER: VILLAGE SHOPKEEPER

THOMAS TURNER

Thomas Turner kept a shop in the village of East Hoathly in Sussex. He was a 'jack of all trades'.

From 1754 to 1765 Thomas kept a diary. This is how we know so much about him. His diary also tells us about life in the 1700s.

Important dates

1729 Thomas was born in Kent.

1735 Thomas' family moved to Sussex.

1750 Thomas became a shopkeeper in East Hoathly.

1753 Thomas married Peggy Slater. Their only child died at the age of five months.

1761 Peggy died.

1765 Thomas married Molly Hick. They had six children. Two of them died when they were babies.

1793 Thomas died and was buried in East Hoathly churchyard.

Shopkeeper
7 July 1755
I paid the gardener 17 pence for some cucumbers I sold for him.

24 December 1755
I paid John Jenner 21 shillings for some hats. I wrote out a bill for Peter Adams. It was almost £9.

I gave two ounces of tobacco for two cheeses.

Looking after the dead
27 December 1761
I went to Lewes to get some brass plates for Mr Calverley's coffin.

28 December 1761
I walked to Whyly with a sheet and shroud for Mr Calverley's coffin.

Teaching children
20 June 1755
My birthday. I treated my scholars to a drink of beer.

17 June 1760
Mr Long went to a cricket match. I took charge of the school for him.

Helping the poor
22 December 1755
St Thomas' Day. I gave 30 poor people a penny each and a drink of beer.

Paying taxes for the village
9 January 1761
I went to Maresfield to pay the land tax for our village. It came to £62.

• Groombridge

SUSSEX

• Uckfield   • Framfield
      • East Hoathly
        • Chiddingly
• Lewes

• Brighton

0 — 10 Miles
0 — 14 km

Having fun
27 May 1756
I went to the fair with my wife. We met Miss Day and some friends. I treated them all to a drink. I spent three shillings.

25 December 1757
Christmas Day. We had boiled beef and plum pudding for dinner.

23 February 1758
I had a party. Some of my friends made me put on my wife's petticoat. I then had to dance barefooted with them!

Source A

Thomas Turner's cottage in East Hoathly.

2.4 STEAM: ALL CHANGE?

Old types of power

There were four types of power before the Industrial Revolution: human muscle power; animal power; wind power and water power. All four had **drawbacks** (see cartoon). The Industrial Revolution meant that a better form of power was needed. The answer was steam power.

The first steam engines

The first steam engine was invented by Thomas Savery in 1698. It was used to pump water out of tin mines. But it was not very safe and often exploded.

In 1712 Thomas Newcomen built a better steam engine. It pumped water out of coal mines, but used too much coal. It was costly to run.

Enter James Watt

James Watt was born in Greenock, Scotland, in 1736. Watt worked at Glasgow University, where he made and repaired scientific instruments.

In 1769 James Watt was asked to mend a model of Newcomen's engine. He noticed all the things wrong with it. Watt then invented a better steam engine, which used less coal than Newcomen's.

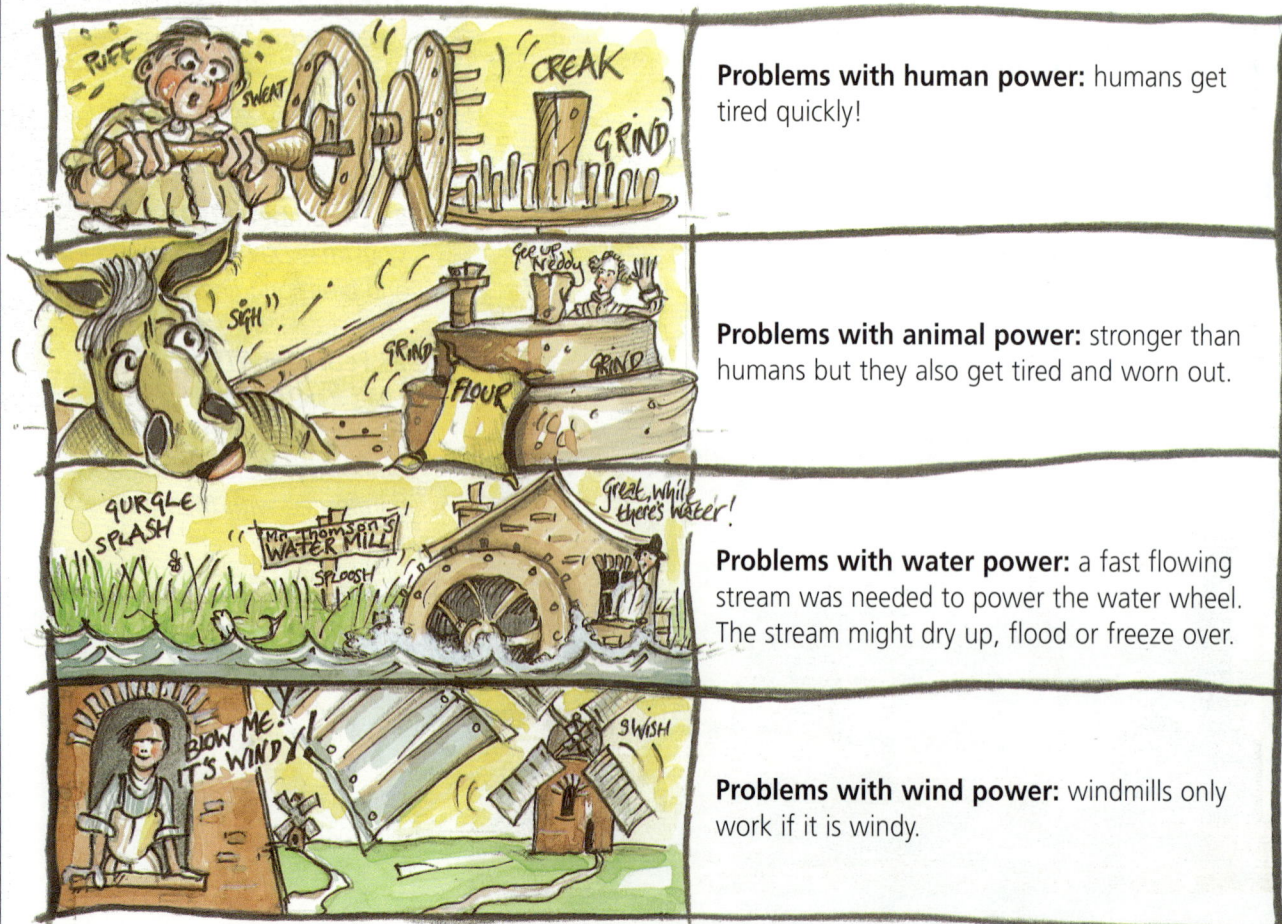

Problems with human power: humans get tired quickly!

Problems with animal power: stronger than humans but they also get tired and worn out.

Problems with water power: a fast flowing stream was needed to power the water wheel. The stream might dry up, flood or freeze over.

Problems with wind power: windmills only work if it is windy.

Rotary motion

Watt joined up with Matthew Boulton, a Birmingham factory owner. In 1781 they invented a steam engine with a driving rod which could drive machines. This was called a **rotary motion** engine. This invention led to the growth of factories and the Industrial Revolution.

Boulton and Watt made a good partnership. Boulton had the money and Watt knew about machines.

Steam engine mad

Now lots of different industries could use steam power, including cotton and wool factories, iron works, pottery works and coal mines.

Source A

Said by Matthew Boulton in the 1780s.

I sell what all the world wants – steam power.

A rotary motion steam engine. Steam makes the driving rod (A) go up and down. The rod was fixed to a small cog (B). This turned a bigger cog (C) which then turned the wheel around.

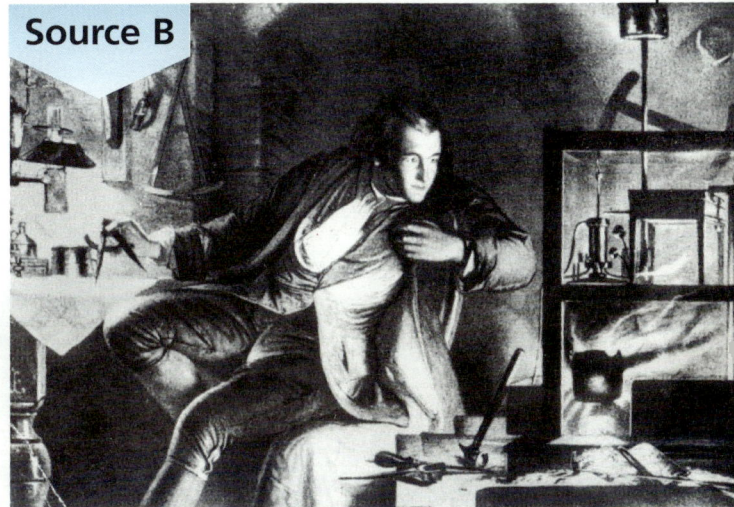

Source B

James Watt, painted in 1869.

Questions

1 Look at the cartoon. What was wrong with each type of power?

2 List the names of three men who built steam engines.

3 Read **Rotary motion**. Why was rotary motion so important?

2.5 LIVING AND WORKING CONDITIONS IN INDUSTRIAL BRITAIN

Finding out about the population

Population means the number of people living in a place.

It is hard to find out the exact population in Britain before 1801. We have to make guesses using **registers** of christenings and burials kept by vicars. These are often inaccurate!

In 1801 the government said there would be a census (count of the population) every ten years. This made it easier to find out the exact size of the population.

A quickly rising population

We do know that Britain's population rose quickly between 1750 and 1900. In 1750 there were about 7 million people living in Britain. This rose to 37 million in 1900 – a very big rise!

Questions

1. Read **A quickly rising population**.
   How many people lived in Britain in:
   a 1750
   b 1900?

2. Read page 39.
   Write down two possible reasons for the rise in population.

3. Look at the diagram on the right-hand side of page 39.
   a What does it tell you about where people lived?
   b Can you explain this?

Source A

The March of Bricks and Mortar, a cartoon drawn in 1829.

Why did the population grow?
This is hard to answer. Here are some possible reasons:

1 More people were being born
- People married earlier and had more children. These children grew up and had children themselves.
- People also had large families, because the children could go to work in the factories and bring in money.

2 People were living longer
- Medicine improved. In 1796 Edward Jenner found out how to **vaccinate** people against smallpox. For many years smallpox had been a killer disease.
- Farming improved. There was plenty of cheap food for people to eat.

Where did all the people live?
Before the Industrial Revolution in the early 1700s, most people lived in small villages. Farming was the main job.

The Industrial Revolution brought factories. People moved into the towns so they could work in the factories. Towns, such as Birmingham, Leeds and Manchester grew very quickly during the 1800s.

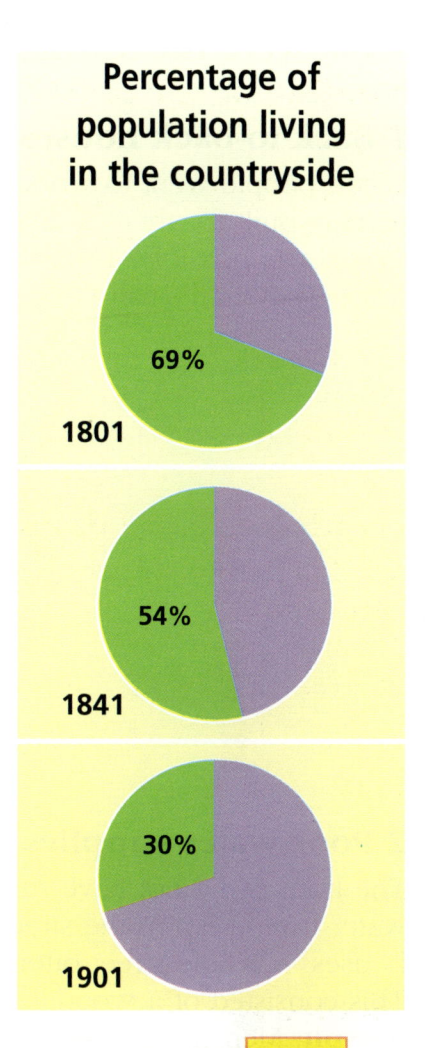

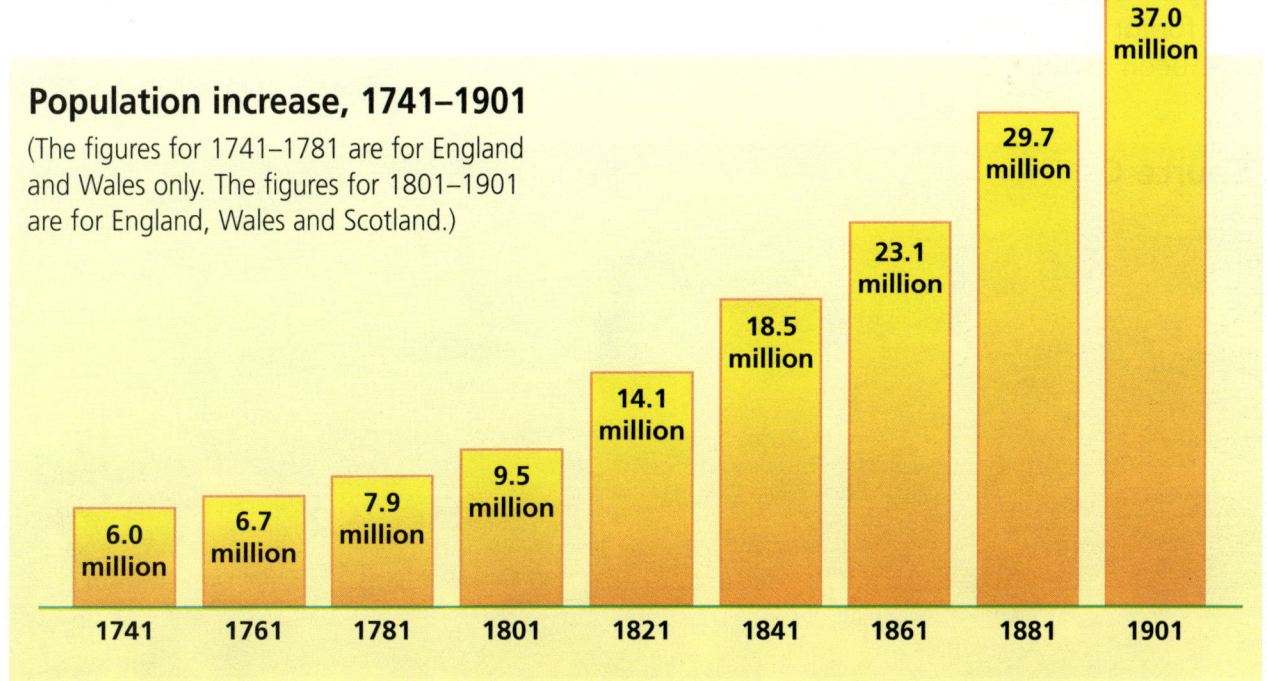

Percentage of population living in the countryside
- 1801: 69%
- 1841: 54%
- 1901: 30%

Population increase, 1741–1901
(The figures for 1741–1781 are for England and Wales only. The figures for 1801–1901 are for England, Wales and Scotland.)

Year	Population
1741	6.0 million
1761	6.7 million
1781	7.9 million
1801	9.5 million
1821	14.1 million
1841	18.5 million
1861	23.1 million
1881	29.7 million
1901	37.0 million

What were the towns like to live in?

1 Back-to-back houses

When people went to work in the factories, houses were quickly built for them to live in. The houses were built as cheaply as possible. They were built back-to-back in long rows. They had small rooms and were cramped.

2 Poor water supplies and few toilets

The houses did not have running water. People took their water from a tap in the street. There were no toilets in the houses. A whole street often shared one outside toilet! This consisted of a wooden seat over a hole called a **cesspit**. Men came to clear out the cess pit. Sometimes they forgot and human dung piled up. The smell must have been awful!

> **Source B**
>
> What Manchester was like in 1832:
>
> Most of the workers' houses have no toilets or proper drainage.
>
> The streets do not have paving slabs. They are muddy and full of rubbish.
>
> In Parliament Street there is just one toilet for 380 people.
>
> Muck flows from the toilet into the street. It must make people ill.

Source C

The city of Manchester in 1850.

The average age of death in four industrial towns in 1840.

The gentry were rich people.

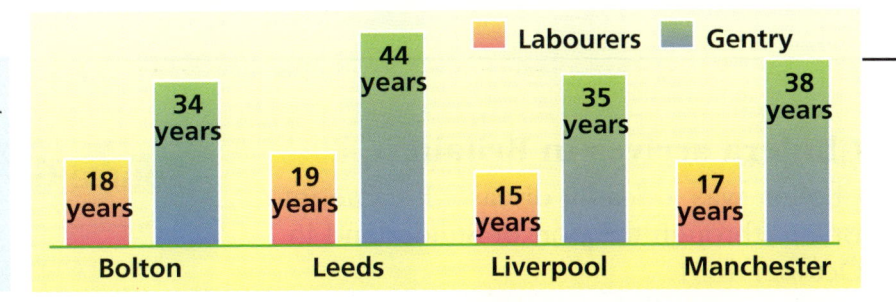

Labourers | Gentry

- Bolton: 18 years / 34 years
- Leeds: 19 years / 44 years
- Liverpool: 15 years / 35 years
- Manchester: 17 years / 38 years

A London street in 1872.

Source D

Questions

1. Read page 40.
Write an essay about what conditions were like in an industrial town. Write in your own words and make up your own sub-headings.

2. Read **Source B** and look at **Source C**.
What do these sources tell you about Manchester in the 1800s?

3. Look at the diagram on this page.
How many reasons can you think of to explain why the gentry lived longer than labourers in the towns?

Source E

The state of the river Aire in Leeds in 1841. People had to drink the water from this river!

Millions of gallons of filth are emptied into the river Aire. It comes from toilets, slaughter houses, factories and chemical works.

Old bandages from the hospital, pig manure and rotten food are also thrown into the river.

Source F

Conditions in Greenock in 1844.

There is a huge dung hill in one street. People buy the dung for manure. Filthy liquid from the dung runs all over the pavement.

People in the nearby houses have to keep their food covered. If it is left uncovered, flies from the dung hill swarm all over it.

Cholera arrives in Britain

Cholera was a deadly disease. It came into Britain through the port of Sunderland in October 1831.

The port was closed but this did not stop the cholera spreading across Britain.

Cholera was spread by infected water and caused terrible pain. People at the time did not know the real causes of cholera.

Between 1831 and 1832, over 50,000 people died from cholera in Britain. There were further outbreaks in 1848, 1854 and 1867.

Source G

From an article in a Sunderland newspaper, just before cholera broke out in 1831.

The signs of cholera:

At first there is giddiness, sickness, and cramp. This is followed by diarrhoea. The face shrinks and the eyes sink. The face, neck, hands and feet turn purple and then black.

There is no cure at the moment. But we are certain the doctors will soon find a cure.

How cholera spread from India to England.

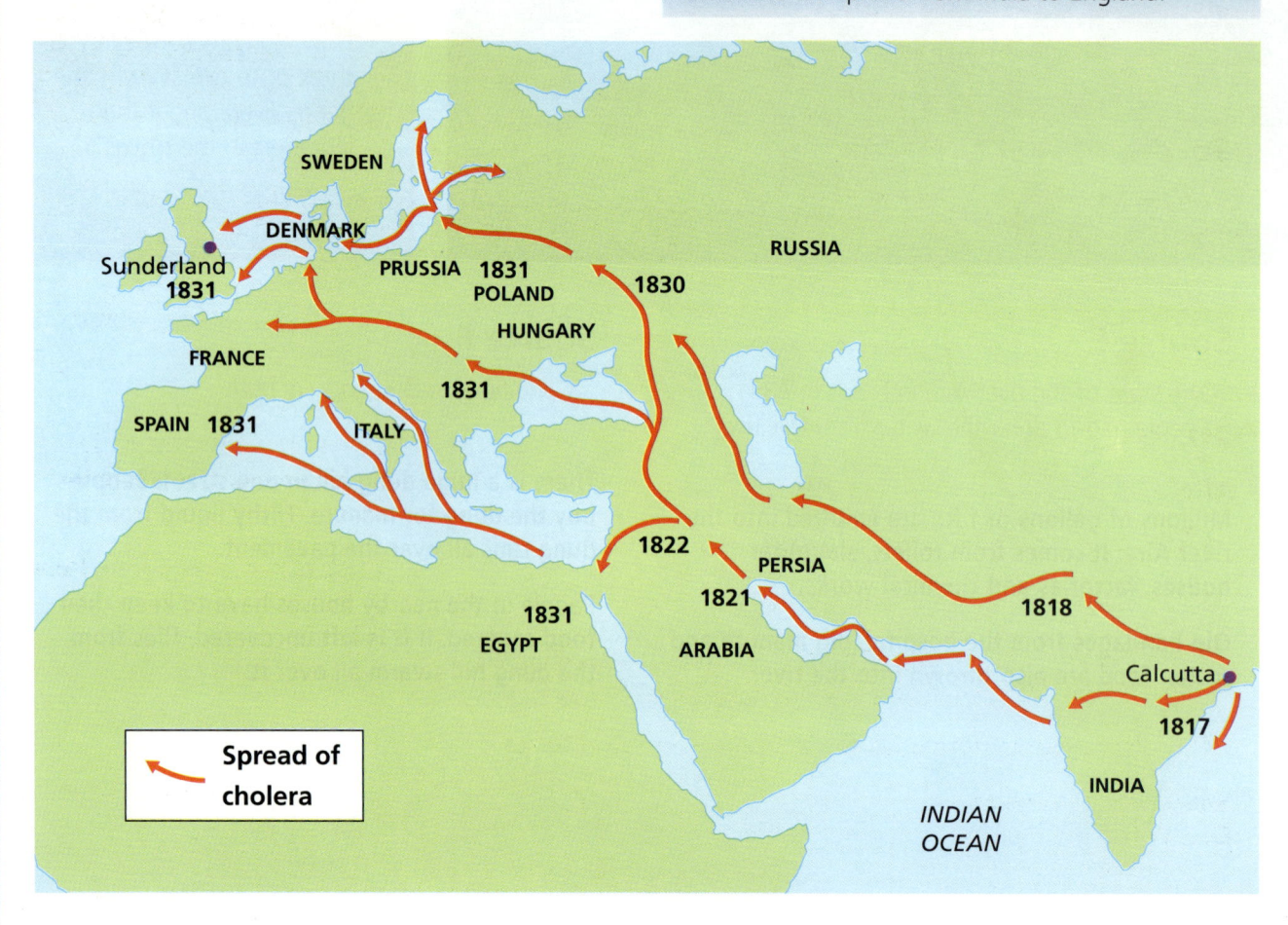

Source H

A Court for King Cholera, a cartoon from 1840. It shows the filth which some people lived in.

Source I

From a letter to Lord Londonderry from his doctor, J. Brown. Londonderry owned a coal mine. When the cholera came to Sunderland he was not allowed to export his coal. Here Dr Brown is saying that the outbreak of cholera was not as serious as people made out.

Dear Lord Londonderry,

After a lot of thought this is what I think about cholera.

1 Cholera has not come from a foreign country.

2 The disease has now stopped spreading.

3 It is the poor who usually catch cholera. They live in filth and are already weak from drinking too much alcohol.

4 Cholera is not infectious, so there is no need to stop trade.

Your obedient servant
Dr J. Brown

Questions

1 Read **Cholera arrives in Britain** and look at the map.
   a Where did the cholera come from?
   b Where and when did it first enter Britain?
   c How was it spread?
   d How many people did it kill in 1831–2?

2 Read **Source G**. What was it like to have cholera?

3 Read **Source I**.
   a In what ways was Dr Brown wrong about cholera?
   b Why might he have said these wrong things about cholera?

Source J

From a report into living conditions in Leeds, printed in 1842.

Disease is more common in the dirtiest streets where the poor live.

Twice as many people die from cholera in filthy areas as in cleaner ones.

43

The coming of factories

In the early 1700s people made cloth in their homes. They used small hand-worked machines. This way of working was called the domestic system.

In 1769 Richard Arkwright built a spinning machine. It needed water to power it and was much too big to fit into a cottage. So Arkwright built a mill (factory) at Cromford in Derbyshire. This was the start of the factory system. Soon others copied his idea.

In 1785 Edmund Cartwright invented a power loom for weaving. It was driven by steam.

It was not long before there were hundreds of cotton and woollen factories using steam power.

Working conditions in the factories

The first factories were not pleasant to work in. The hours were long and the wages were low.

The steam engines made the air hot and stuffy. There were no safety guards on the machines. People sometimes had their fingers chopped off by moving machinery.

Source K

TO
Journeymen Spinners
Wanted Immediately,
From Eighty to One Hundred
MULE SPINNERS,
For a New Mill and other Mills, in Great Bolton, which New Mill is complete with new Machinery now ready gaited, and will commence running on Monday Morning next, adjoining to which Mills are a Number of Cottages, for the convenience and accommodation of Spinners: liberal Wages will be given and constant employ.
For further particulars apply to Messrs. ORMROD and HARDCASTLE, of Bolton aforesaid, Cotton Spinners.

A mill in Bolton advertising for workers, 1816.

Source M

This picture comes from a novel about an orphan boy working in a factory. It was written in 1840.

Source L

Fines in a Manchester cotton mill, 1823.

Having a window open	1 shilling
Being dirty at work	1 shilling
Whistling	1 shilling
Being five minutes late	1 shilling

Laws which made factory conditions better

Factory Act 1833: Children under 9 not allowed to work in mills.

Factory Act 1847: Women and young people not to work more than ten hours a day.

Factory Act 1874: No worker to work more than 56.5 hours a week.

Questions

1 Read **Working conditions in the factories**. What was it like inside a factory?

2 Read **Punishments**.
   a Why were children used in the factories?
   b What punishments were used?

3 Read **Were factory owners cruel?** Why were punishments used?

4 **Source M** is from a novel. Novels are long stories which have been made up. Would you trust this source as evidence about factory conditions?

Punishments

Children were used a lot in the factories. They were cheap and could get under the machines to clean them.

The factory owners wanted to make a profit. **Overseers** (foremen) walked up and down to make sure that the work was being done properly.

Anyone caught breaking the rules would be fined or strapped.

Were the factory owners cruel?

Many history books say that the factory owners were cruel. But this is not completely fair.

1 The workers were not used to set hours. They were bad timekeepers and had to be trained to turn up on time. This is why there were fines for lateness.

2 Not all factory owners punished their workers. Some, like Robert Owen, treated their workers well.

3 Some factory owners, like John Fielden, wanted to reform (improve) working conditions. They asked Parliament to pass laws to do this.

Source N

A day in the life of a mill girl, 1842.

4.30 am Gets up.

5.30 am Starts work at the factory.

7.30 am A quick breakfast.

Midday: Stops the machine and cleans it. Goes home for some soup and bread.

1.00 pm Back at work.

7.00 pm Stops work. Cleans the machine.

7.30 pm Goes home.

It has been a 14-hour day. It is a six-day week.

2.6 MARIA WOOLF: CHOLERA VICTIM

Source A

The marriage certificate of George Woolf and Maria Mordecai, September 1842.

Maria Mordecai and George Woolf were married on 28 September 1842 in London. Maria and George were Jews whose families had come to Britain from central Europe to escape ill-treatment. The wedding was attended by George's brothers and sisters, his father, Joseph, and mother, Alcry. Maria's father, Jonas, was also there.

Cholera

On 18 April 1844 Maria had a son, called Joseph. The Woolf family took their water from a nearby stream. This was the same stream into which household waste was dumped. It was a perfect place for cholera to breed. In June 1849 disaster struck the family.

Source B

This drawing of George Woolf was made in 1858 from an earlier, lost portrait.

Source C

Joseph Woolf, the son of George and Maria, drawn in 1858.

Source D

No.	When and where died	Name and surname	Sex	Age	Occupation	Cause of death	Signature, description, and residence of informant	When registered	Signature of registrar
100	Eighteenth June 1849 106 Shoe Lane St. Brides	Maria Woolf	Female	32 years	Wife of George Woolf Accountant	Diarrhoea 8 days Cholera 4 days Premature Labour 32 hours Exhaustion Certified	G. Woolf Present at the Death 106 Shoe Lane London	Nineteenth June 1849	William Nason Registrar

Registration District: West London
1849. DEATH in the Sub-district of West London in the City of London.

The death certificate of Maria Woolf, June 1849.

Source E

A mourning ring, made after Maria Woolf's death. It contains woven strands of Maria's hair. The ring would have been worn by her husband, or another relative, in memory of Maria.

Maria dies

Maria Woolf, who was pregnant again, caught cholera. Her illness made her go into labour too early, but within eight days she and her baby were dead.

George Woolf and his son, Joseph, survived the cholera, but George died two years later from tuberculosis in 1851. Joseph was brought up by his Aunt Julia and Uncle Joel. He died in 1911.

Source F

Kate Vaughan-Williams, a modern doctor, said this about Maria Woolf's death.

Maria probably had cholera for eight days. She would have had serious pain in her stomach; smelly, explosive, watery diarrhoea and a high fever. All this would have caused early labour. She was probably bleeding heavily, too.

Eventually her body would not have been able to circulate blood any more and then she died.

Questions

1. Read page 46.
   a. When were Maria and George married?
   b. Why had their families come to Britain?

2. Read **Cholera**, **Maria dies** and **Source F**.
   a. Why do you think Maria caught cholera?
   b. What happened to her?
   c. What happened to George and Joseph?

3. What can you find out about Maria Woolf and her family from the marriage certificate and Maria's death certificate?

2.7 BRADFORD WOOLCOMBERS: DANGEROUS AND DEADLY WORK

Source A

Bradford in the 1840s. The first mill (factory) in Bradford for spinning wool was built in 1803. By 1840 Bradford had over thirty spinning mills.

The worsted industry

Bradford is in West Yorkshire. In the 1800s it was important for the making of **worsted**, a type of woollen cloth.

Whole families were involved in this industry. The men worked at home combing the raw wool. The women and children worked in the mills. Here the fibres were spun and woven into worsted cloth using big machines.

Woolcombers and their families lived in cramped houses next to the mills. Often the whole family lived in just one room. This was also the room where the woolcombers did their work

The growth of Bradford

1801: 13,000 people
1821: 26,000 people
1841: 67,000 people

Making worsted

1 Raw wool was combed into long fibres.
2 The long fibres were spun into strong thread.
3 The thread was woven into worsted cloth.

How was wool combed?

The men heated up large metal combs on charcoal stoves. The combs had lots of sharp metal teeth. When one comb was hot it was fastened to a wooden post. The men threw a big handful of wool on to the teeth. Then they pulled another hot comb through the wool. This unravelled the wool into long, straight fibres.

It was a very dirty and smelly job. The stoves gave off fumes and the wool was smelly and greasy. At night the same room was used for cooking, eating and sleeping.

Higher wages, please!

The woolcombers worked for the mill owners. The owners made a lot of money from making worsted cloth, but they paid low wages to the woolcombers.

The woolcombers thought this was unfair. In 1825 they went on strike for higher wages. They got nowhere. Instead the mill owners put their wages down!

Enter Samuel Lister

In 1843 Samuel Lister invented a woolcombing machine. It could comb wool much quicker than by hand. Mill owners bought the new machines in large numbers and so fewer workers were needed. Lister became very rich.

Some woolcombers took jobs operating the new machines. But most of them were thrown out of work. They found it very difficult to get another job in Bradford. Thousands of woolcombers faced starvation. Some of them emigrated to make a new start in life.

By 1858 there were no hand woolcombers left in Bradford.

Source B

Some woolcombers advertised for new jobs.

Wanted: Jobs as goods porters are wanted by 100 strong, active, honest and hardworking woolcombers, aged between 22 and 40 years old.

Source C

From a report on the living conditions of woolcombers in Bradford in 1845.

Pinfold Street: Filthy yards and cellars. People are crowded together. The fumes from the charcoal make people ill. A number of children have just died of fever.

Mary Gate: Upper room has three charcoal stoves worked by six people. There are two beds in the same room where four people sleep. The room is smelly and hot.

Nelson Court: Many woolcombers live here in cellars. They are filthy and there is no drainage. A terrible stink comes from a nearby sewer. These cellars are unfit to live in.

Questions

1. Read **How was wool combed?** and **Source C**.
   What was it like to live in a woolcomber's house in Bradford?

2. Read **Higher wages, please!**
   a How did the mill owners treat the woolcombers?
   b What did the woolcombers do?

3. Read **Enter Samuel Lister**.
   a What did Lister do in 1843?
   b Why was this bad for the woolcombers?
   c What happened to the woolcombers?

2.8 TITUS SALT: A CARING MILL OWNER

A grand funeral

Titus Salt (1803–76) was one of the most popular mill owners in Yorkshire.

His funeral took place on 6 January 1877. Bradford came to a standstill. All the factories closed down and flags flew at half-mast.

A crowd of 100,000 people lined the streets to watch the funeral procession.

The funeral was attended by lots of important people, including MPs, lords and mill owners.

Everyone, rich and poor, wanted to pay their last respects to Titus Salt.

Bradford – a growing town

In 1800 Bradford was just a small town. But by 1850 it was a town of 129 factories and 100,000 people.

Cheap houses were quickly built for all the people. Living conditions were bad. There were no proper sewers and people had to share outside toilets.

There was overcrowding and lots of disease. Clouds of smoke from the factory chimneys hung over the town.

Titus Salt starts out

In 1834 Titus Salt opened his first worsted mill. He went on to make a lot of money.

All his mills were fitted with combing, spinning and weaving machines.

Salt made a lot of worsted very quickly and sold it cheaply.

Source A

A photograph of Titus Salt (1803–76).

Source B

Bradford in the 1840s, written by a modern historian.

The Bradford Canal which ran through the town was like an open sewer. It was called the 'River Stink' by the local people.

Factories poured out smoke from their chimneys. It made people cough and blackened clothes and buildings.

Many people were dead by the time they were twenty.

There were lots of marches and meetings protesting about long working hours.

Source C

These dresses were made from alpaca in 1862. They were very popular. Queen Victoria had many dresses made from Salt's alpaca cloth.

Alpaca

In 1836 Salt went to Liverpool. He found some wool which looked different. It was goats' wool from Peru in South America. It was called alpaca.

A new kind of cloth

Salt bought the alpaca and took it back to Yorkshire. He found a way of weaving alpaca with cotton and silk to make a light, shiny cloth. It was made into dresses, which became very popular (see Source C).

A clever move

Salt did not want anyone else copying him. To stop them he bought up all the alpaca as soon as it arrived in England. By doing this only he could make the new cloth.

Salt made a fortune from selling alpaca.

Source D

Written by a historian in 1997.

In 1834, about 12,000 kilos of alpaca came into Britain. This went up to 2 million kilos in 1840. Alpaca cloth was very popular.

A good master

Salt was good to his workers. He paid them good wages and did not sack them when trade was bad. In return his workers worked hard for him.

In the early 1850s Salt built a new factory away from the filth of Bradford. You can read about this in Unit 2.9.

Questions

1. Read **Titus Salt starts out**.
   a. When did Salt open his first mill?
   b. What sort of cloth did he make?

2. Read **A new kind of cloth**.
   a. What was the new cloth made by Salt?
   b. Why did he make a lot of money from it?

3. Read **A good master**.
   What made Titus Salt a good master?

4. Read **A grand funeral**.
   a. What was it like in Bradford on the day of Salt's funeral?
   b. Why do you think people wanted to pay their last respects to Salt?

2.9 SALTAIRE: A GENTLE PRISON?

Salt's new mill

Salt built a new mill and village for his workers at Saltaire, three miles north of Bradford.

The mill had combing, spinning and weaving machines all under one roof. It was bigger than any mill in Bradford.

A party!

The new mill was opened on 20 September 1853, which was Salt's fiftieth birthday. He held a big party for over 3000 workers.

New houses

Salt built new houses for his workers near to the mill.

The houses were well-built with a yard and an outside toilet.

Salt believed that people worked harder if they had good houses to live in.

By 1871 Salt had built 824 houses for about 5000 workers.

He also built a church, a school, a hospital and houses for the elderly.

The streets were named after members of Salt's family, such as Ada Street and George Street.

Source A

A drawing of Salt's mill done in 1885.

Source B

Saltaire in more recent times. The houses in Ada Street (top) were built for workers. Those in George Street (bottom) were for foremen.

Source C

52

Source D

Roberts Park at Saltaire in 1874. Many sports were enjoyed here, including archery, swimming and cricket.

Gambling, swearing, stone-throwing and dogs were not allowed in the park.

Spare time

Salt made sure the workers had plenty to do in their spare time. He did not want them drinking or gambling. So he provided other things for them to do instead.

1 Clubs. Salt refused to build any pubs in Saltaire. Instead, he gave the workers money to start up clubs. For example, there was a cricket club and a gardening club.

2 The Institute. This was a large building with a concert hall, a library, a reading room, billiards room and smoking room.

Salt wanted his workers to spend their time in the Institute. They could read and educate themselves here. It cost very little to join and it soon had over 1000 members.

Was Saltaire a gentle prison?

Salt had a lot of power over his workers. Workers had to follow the rules or get the sack. Those who were sacked also lost their house in the village. So Salt's workers were very obedient. They did not go on strike and behaved well.

Some people said Saltaire was like a prison because the rules were so strict.

But Salt's workers did not think of Saltaire as a prison. They wanted to be there and were happy to follow the strict rules.

Questions

1. Look back at **Bradford – a growing town** on page 50.
   Why do you think Salt wanted to move away from Bradford?

2. Read **Salt's new mill** and look at **Source A**.
   What was the new mill like?

3. Read **New houses**.
   Why did Salt build good houses for his workers?

4. Read **Spare time** and look at **Source D**.
   a. Why did Salt want the workers to have plenty to do?
   b. What could the workers do in their spare time?

5. Read **Was Saltaire a gentle prison?**
   Would you have liked to have worked for Titus Salt? Give reasons for your answer.

2.10 SAMUEL GREG: A RISK TAKER?

The cotton industry
In the late 1700s the making of cotton cloth was the most important industry in Britain.

New spinning machines had been invented. They could spin cotton thread quickly and in large amounts. For anyone with money to spend and willing to take a risk, there were big profits to be made.

Who was Samuel Greg?
Greg was a Manchester merchant. In 1783 he decided to build his own cotton spinning mill. He thought it was worth the risk. The question was: Where could he build it?

Greg rode around looking for a place to build his new mill.

Styal – a suitable site
One day Greg visited the village of Styal, ten miles south of Manchester.

He noticed there was a fast flowing river which would be able to power a water wheel.

The water wheel, in turn, would then drive the spinning machines. It was just the place to build a mill.

In 1784 Greg built his new mill at Styal. It was called Quarry Bank Mill.

Source A

Samuel Greg as a young man.

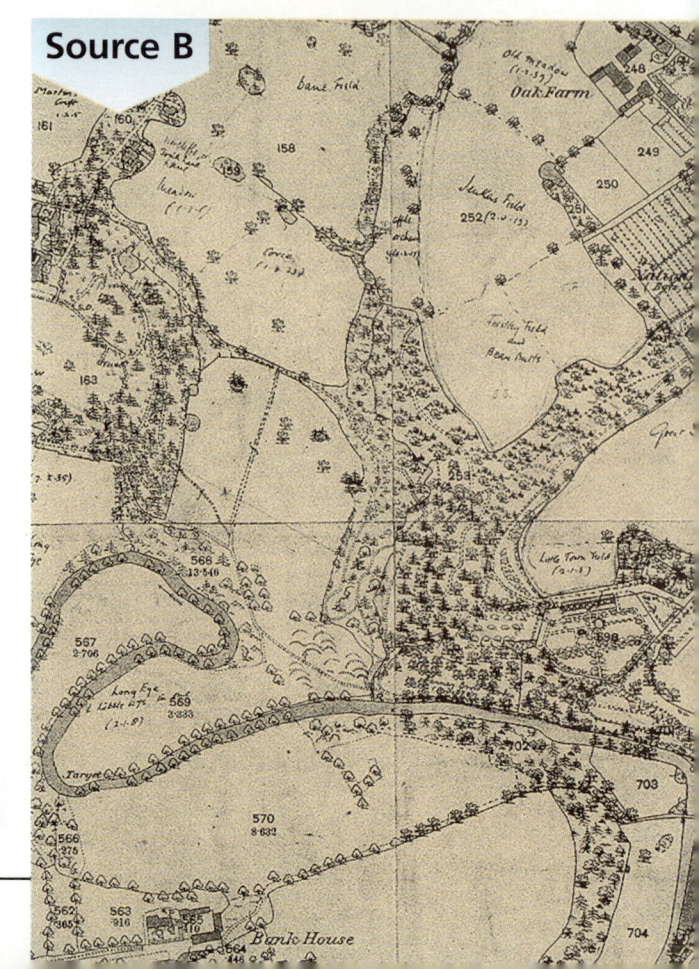

Source B

An eighteenth-century map of the area around Styal.

Finding workers

The new mill cost £16,000 to build and equip. But Greg had to find people to work in the mill. Styal was a small village of farmers. No one had ever seen a mill before, let alone worked in one!

By 1790, Greg had found 183 adults and children to work in the mill. Where did they come from?

1. Some were local people.
2. Some were from Greg's other mill in Derbyshire.
3. Some were from mills in Lancashire.
4. Most of his workers were children from workhouses.

Greg built an Apprentice House for the children to live in and cottages for the adult workers.

A risk taker?

Greg might have had money but he did not know much about spinning cotton! So building a new mill was a risk. He could easily have made a loss.

But Greg was clever. He brought in a partner who knew all about spinning cotton.

Together they made the mill bigger and bought more machinery.

By 1800 Greg was very rich. The risk *had* been worth taking!

Source C

Quarry Bank Mill today.

Why a mill was built at Styal
- Greg had the money.
- New machines had been invented.
- There was a river for power.
- People wanted cotton goods.
- Greg was willing to take a risk.

Questions

1. Read **The cotton industry**.
   Why did Greg think it might be a good idea to build a cotton mill?

2. Read **Styal – a suitable site** and look at the map.
   Why was Styal a good place to build a mill?

3. Read **A risk taker?**
   How did things work out for Greg?

2.11 ESTHER PRICE: A RUNAWAY APPRENTICE

Child labour

Many children worked in cotton spinning mills in the early 1800s. Why was this?

1 They were cheaper than adults.
2 They were easy to train.
3 They were small enough to clean under the machines.
4 They had nimble fingers and could mend broken threads.

A lot of children worked at Quarry Bank Mill. They came from the workhouse in Liverpool. The children were employed as **apprentices**.

Esther Price was one of these children.

Esther Price arrives at Quarry Bank Mill

Esther Price was born in Liverpool on 8 March 1820. When Esther was a young child she was sent to the Liverpool workhouse.

In 1833 Esther was sent to work as an apprentice at Quarry Bank Mill. She was examined by a doctor to make sure she was strong enough to stand the work.

Esther lived in the Apprentice House next to the mill.

Source A

A girl cleaning under a spinning machine. Quarry Bank Mill had machines like this.

Esther Price's baptism certificate.

Source B

Esther gets into trouble

Mr and Mrs Timperley were in charge of the Apprentice House. They were not very good at controlling the children. There were lots of fights.

In November 1835 Esther injured another apprentice in a fight. She was sent to court.

Esther runs away

In August 1836 Esther asked her boss if she could visit her father in Liverpool. Her boss would not let her go. So Esther ran away without telling anyone. She was away from the mill for ten days.

Esther is punished

When she got back Esther was punished. She was kept alone in a room in the Apprentice House.

She was not allowed to talk to anyone. The windows were boarded up so she could not run away again.

Esther had to sleep on the floor. She was given milk, bread and porridge to eat.

Esther stays on

In 1838 Esther's apprenticeship came to end. She was free to leave Quarry Bank Mill. But she stayed on at the mill for the rest of her working life.

Source C

A modern photograph of the Apprentice House where Esther lived.

Questions

1. Read **Child labour**.
   a. Why were children used in cotton mills?
   b. Where did the children at Quarry Bank come from?

2. What does **Source B** tell us about Esther Price?

3. Read **Esther runs away**. Why did Esther run away from the mill?

4. Read **Esther is punished**. What punishment was given to Esther?

5. Why do you think Esther stayed at the mill after her apprenticeship was over?

2.12 DOWN THE PIT

Before the Industrial Revolution large amounts of coal were not needed. Coal could be mined from near the surface.

Bell pit.

Adit mine.

The Industrial Revolution meant lots of coal was needed. The surface coal was soon used up. So deep shafts had to be dug into the ground (see picture below).

A dangerous job

Deep mining was a dangerous job. The mines flooded if there was a lot of rain. Sometimes roofs caved in.

There was no fresh air and the coal gave off a gas. This exploded if it came into contact with a flame.

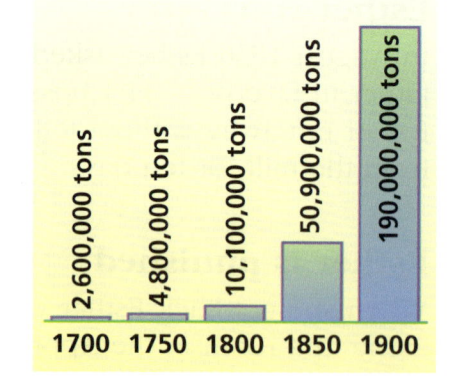

Getting fresh air into the mines

A second shaft was dug and a furnace built at the bottom.

Stale air was warmed and it rose up out of the mine. Fresh air then came down the first shaft.

Doors were built underground to control the flow of fresh air. Children called trappers opened the doors to let trucks of coal through.

Why more coal was needed

- To heat homes.
- To power steam engines in factories.
- To heat iron furnaces.
- To drive steam-powered trains.

1700	2,600,000 tons
1750	4,800,000 tons
1800	10,100,000 tons
1850	50,900,000 tons
1900	190,000,000 tons

Coal production in Britain, 1700–1900.

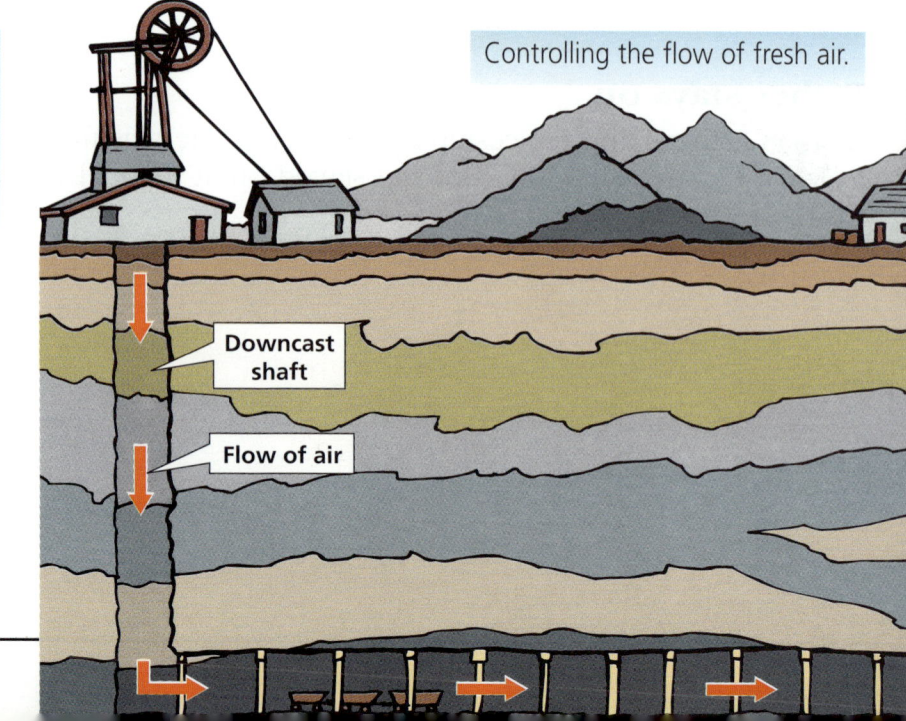

Controlling the flow of fresh air.

Source A

The job of a trapper. From a government report, 1842.

Trappers sit in a little hole and open and shut the doors. They sit in the dark and damp for twelve hours a day. They are aged between five and ten.

Questions

1 Why was more coal needed?

2 Read **A dangerous job**. What were the dangers of deep mining?

3 Read **Sources A, B** and **C**. What do you think it was like to be a trapper?

Source B

Said in 1842 by Lord Londonderry, a coal mine owner.

Government inspectors trick the children into giving the answers they want.

A trapper's job is not lonely or dull. Every five minutes someone passes through his door and has a word.

Trappers are cheerful and happy in their work.

Protection against gas

1 Canaries. Miners took canaries with them into the mines as a way of finding out whether gas was present. If the canary dropped dead, they knew there was gas about. It was time to get out of the mine.

2 Humphrey Davy's safety lamp. In 1815 Humphrey Davy invented a safety lamp. The flame had a wire gauze (mesh) around it. This gauze stopped gas from reaching the flame. The safety lamp was a great help to the miners. It helped to stop some of the explosions.

Source C

Said by a retired miner in 1912.

I remember my first day working as a trapper in a mine. My father made me a hole to sit in.

A lot of miners passed through. I pulled the door open with a piece of string. They spoke to me and told me to be careful.

The foreman was a big man. He was very stern. He had a stick and said, 'If you go to sleep and don't keep that door shut, you'll be in trouble.'

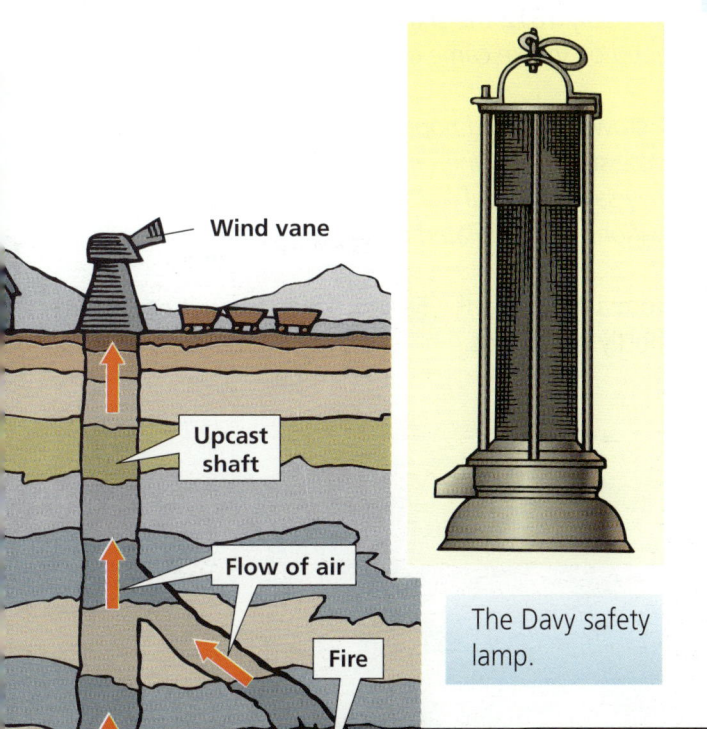

Wind vane

Upcast shaft

Flow of air

Fire

The Davy safety lamp.

Pit villages

As more coal was needed, lots of new coal mines (pits) were opened. Villages grew around the mines.

The miners and their families lived in the villages.

Pit villages were very close communities. Everyone knew each other. People stuck together because mining was so hard and dangerous.

The fear of an explosion

People lived in fear of an explosion under the ground. This was likely to happen at any time. On 25 May 1812 there was a terrible explosion at Felling pit in the north-east of England.

Source D

Some of the miners killed at Felling pit in 1812.

Name	Job	Age
Thomas Craggs	Hewer	36
Thomas Craggs	Trapper	9
William Dixon	Hewer	35
John Pearson	Hewer	64
Joseph Gordon	Trapper	10
Robert Gordon	Hewer	40
Thomas Gordon	Trapper	8

Explosion at Felling pit!

The coal mine (pit) at Felling was opened in May 1811.

On 25 May 1812 there was a terrible explosion. The ground trembled half a mile away.

Lumps of coal, wood and bodies were blown up the shaft.

It was dreadful. Roads and paths were covered with coal and bits of machinery.

People from the village rushed to the mine, hoping their loved ones had survived.

Straight after the explosion some brave men went down the mine to see what had happened. But it was too dark to see anything. A fire was burning underground and they had to come out. They only managed to rescue 32 men out of a total of 120. Three died later.

The mine owners covered the shaft so that the fire would burn itself out.

On 7 July 1812 the shaft was re-opened. A great cloud of smoke came out.

A crowd gathered hoping that the missing miners were still alive. When men went down the mine they saw an awful sight. There were twisted wagons and mutilated bodies everywhere.

From a report on the Felling explosion, written shortly afterwards.

Source E

An explosion at a coal mine near Barnsley in 1866.

Source F

A trapper at work. From a government report of 1842.

Jobs down the mine

Trapper: a child who opened and closed ventilation doors.
Hewer: a miner who dug out coal with a pick axe.
Putter: a young miner who pushed tubs of coal to the shaft bottom.

Source G

A miner called Michael Smith scratched these words on his water bottle. He was trapped underground by an explosion at Seaham Colliery in 1880. He died along with 163 others.

Dear Margaret

There are 40 of us trapped down here. Some men are singing hymns, but my thoughts are on my little Michael.

My dear wife. God save you and the children. Pray for me. Farewell, my last thoughts are with you. I hope we meet in Heaven.

Questions

1. Read **Pit villages**.
   What do you think it was like to live in a pit village?

2. Read **Jobs down the mine**.
   What was done by:
   a a trapper
   b a hewer
   c a putter?

3. Read **Explosion at Felling pit**.
   a Write a paragraph in your own words about the explosion.
   b Work out how many miners died.

4. Read **Source D**.
   a How old were the trappers who died?
   b Which of the dead miners do you think were related?

5. 'Davy's safety lamp (1815) put an end to explosions in mines.' Do you agree or disagree? Use evidence from the sources on this page to back up your answer.

61

2.13 GETTING ABOUT

Poor roads

In the early 1700s the roads were very poor. They were muddy in the winter and rutted in the summer. Goods were carried by packhorses and big wagons. People travelled on horseback or walked.

Turnpike Trusts

Turnpike Trusts were set up to improve the roads. These were groups who took over a stretch of road and kept it in good condition.

Travellers had to stop at a gate and were charged a **toll** (fee) for using the road. The tolls were collected by a toll-keeper who lived in a house next to the gate. The tolls were used to repair the road.

Road engineers

The two most famous road engineers were John Macadam (1756–1836) and Thomas Telford (1757–1834). They built hundreds of miles of good roads for the Turnpike Trusts.

Stagecoaches and mail coaches

Better roads meant that long-distance travellers could use wheeled coaches.

People travelled in stagecoaches which went between big towns. The stagecoaches ran to a timetable, stopping at inns along the way. Here the stable lads changed the horses while the passengers had a meal.

In 1784 the Post Office started using coaches to carry the mail as well as passengers. They also carried an armed guard.

Source A

This painting from 1839 shows a stagecoach passing through a turnpike at night.

Source B

A road designed by John Macadam.

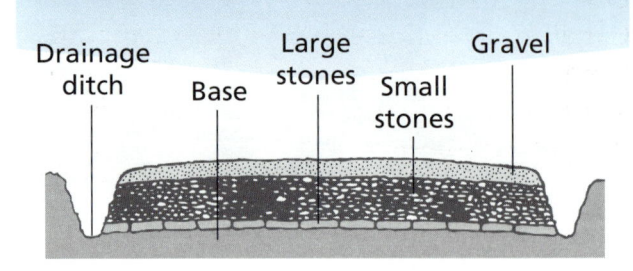

Drainage ditch — Base — Large stones — Small stones — Gravel

Source C

Types of road in 1838.

There were 22,000 miles of turnpiked roads. Average speed was 7 mph.

There were 100,000 miles of unturnpiked roads. Average speed was 3 mph.

Canals

Even with better roads, it was still hard to move heavy goods around.

Rivers and the sea were used to move goods such as coal and iron. The trouble was that many factories were not near a river or the sea.

Canals were better. They were man-made waterways and could be specially built to link factories to rivers and ports. Canals carried coal, stone, wood and clay.

The first canal was the Sankey Cut in 1757. In 1761 the Duke of Bridgewater paid for the Bridgewater Canal. It carried coal from his mine at Worsley to Manchester.

Canal mania

In the 1790s some business people went mad on canal-building. They thought they could make money out of them. But canals were costly to build. Some canals failed and lost money.

One successful canal was the Grand Trunk Canal. It carried Josiah Wedgwood's pottery from his Stoke factory to market. The smooth canal meant that the pottery did not get smashed.

Canals in 1830. Canals linked most places with the ports of London, Bristol, Liverpool and Hull.

Source D
An advert in a Birmingham newspaper, 1811.

Thomas Coleman Canal Carrier:

Boats loaded daily to go to Manchester and Liverpool.

Boats also loaded for Lincolnshire, Hull and Newcastle.

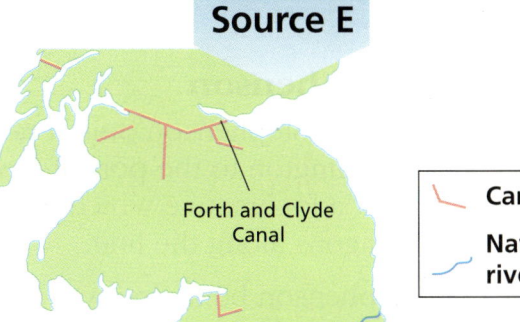

Source E

Questions

1. Read **Poor roads**.
   What were roads like in the early 1700s?

2. Read **Turnpike Trusts**.
   What were Turnpike Trusts?

3. Read **Canals**.
   What sort of goods did canals carry?

4. Read **Canal mania**.
   a. What was canal mania?
   b. Why do you think Josiah Wedgwood was pleased with the Grand Trunk Canal?

The first railways

The first railways were used in coal mines in the late 1700s. Horses pulled wagons of coal along wooden tracks.

The first moving steam engine (a locomotive) was built in 1804 by Richard Trevithick. It pulled some wagons along an iron railway track in South Wales.

George Stephenson

In 1825 George Stephenson built a railway line from Darlington to the port of Stockton. He also built a locomotive which was used to pull coal wagons along the line.

In 1830 Stephenson built a railway line between Liverpool and Manchester. The line was opened by the Prime Minister, the Duke of Wellington.

William Huskisson, the MP for Liverpool, was knocked down by a train at the opening. He later died. Not many people were bothered by this. They were more excited about the new railway! The Liverpool–Manchester railway line was a big success.

Liverpool–Manchester Railway

	1831	1835
Passengers carried	450,000	475,000
Goods carried	100,000 tons	155,000 tons

Railway mania

People soon realised that there was a lot of money to be made from railways. They could be used to carry goods and passengers. In the 1840s people went mad on building new railways. It was called the railway **mania**. By 1855, over 8000 miles of railway track had been built.

- Canal transport would end.
- There would be soot everywhere.
- Turnpike Trusts would go bust.
- Fox hunting would be ruined.
- Milking would be affected.
- Women would **miscarry**.
- Sparks would cause fires.
- There would be railway tracks everywhere.
- Fast travel would send people mad.

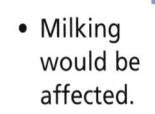

Arguments against the railway at the time.

Source F

The Railway Station painted in 1862 by William Powell Frith.

Britain's railways in 1852.

Questions

1. Read **The first railways**.
   a. Where were railways first used?
   b. What did Richard Trevithick build?

2. Read **George Stephenson**.
   Which two railway lines did Stephenson build and when?

3. Read **Railway mania**.
   Why were people keen to build railways?

4. Look at the cartoon.
   Which of the arguments do you think were:
   a. sensible
   b. not sensible?
   Explain your answer.
   c. Why would some people have been frightened of railways?

Source G

The signalling rules which Neele helped to invent.

DANGER STOP

CAUTION

ALL RIGHT

George Neele – railway worker

George Neele (1825–1921) worked all his life on the railways.

In 1862 he became the superintendent (manager) of the London and North Western Railway (LNWR).

The LNWR was the biggest railway company in Britain.

In 1895 George retired. He wrote a book called *Railway Reminiscences*, which was all about his life on the railways.

Here are some of the things George wrote about. George's words are in *italics*.

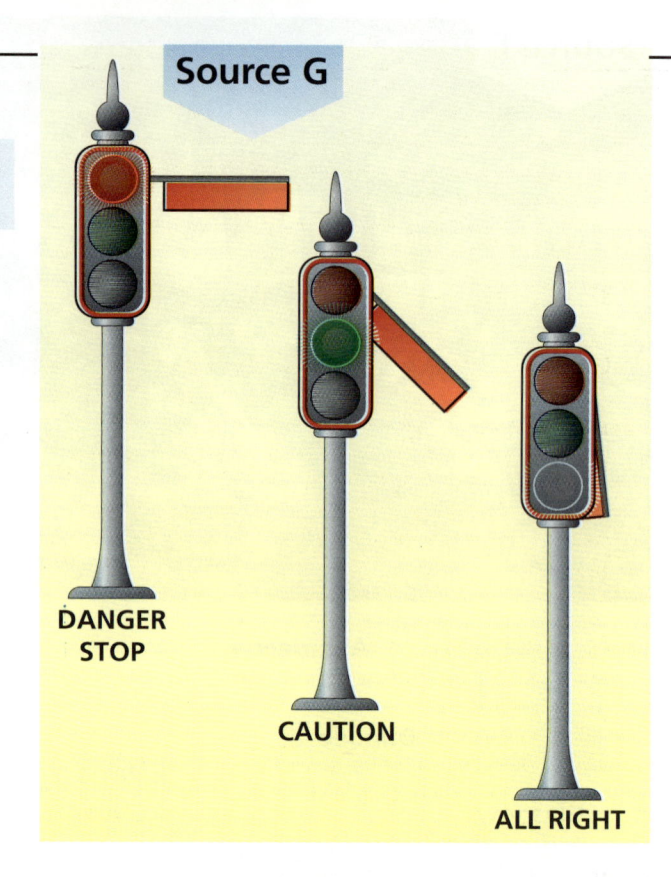

Where's that train?

Stations only knew a train was approaching when they saw the smoke of the engine or heard it whistle. Porters had to be on the platform all the time, watching out for a train coming.

At first stations along a railway line had no way of keeping in touch with each other.

Signals

George Neele helped to invent the signals all railway companies used.

Accident at Abergele!

In 1868 the Irish mail train crashed into four petrol wagons near Abergele in North Wales. George Neele went to investigate the crash.

The Marquis of Hamilton was in a carriage at the back of the mail train. He wrote a letter to *The Times*. George tells us what was in the letter.

The Marquis said that he got off the train straightaway after the crash. The three front carriages and the engine were on fire. Thick smoke rose high into the air.

The crash was so sudden that people were killed instantly. Dead bodies were later found in the carriages. They were burnt and mangled.

A late 19th century locomotive.

Source H

1873: Train wrecked at Wigan!

George wrote about another accident.

For some reason a carriage broke away at Wigan and turned to the left. It took the rest of the train with it. The first eight carriages were wrecked. Many people were killed.

An inquiry was held into the crash. It was almost certainly caused by the train going too fast.

Queen Victoria's train journeys

George Neele often travelled with Queen Victoria on her journeys to and from Scotland. Here he writes about three of these journeys.

1865
At Forfar a worker took a horse-drawn goods wagon across the track just as the Queen's train came into the station. The Queen's train almost hit the wagon. The worker said he had not seen the Queen's train and went on with his work. He wasn't at all bothered about the near miss!

1872
The train stopped briefly at Wigan. I saw the Queen's servant, John Brown, on the platform. It was dark. I asked him if everything was all right. 'No,' he said, 'the Queen says the carriage is shaking like the devil.' I think this was Brown's way of putting it, not the Queen's!

1884
At Oxford the Queen was angry that the lights in her carriage were using gas rather than oil. The gas made the lights too bright. The Queen asked for some oil lights but we did not have any. I had to turn down the gas instead.

Questions

1. Read **George Neele – railway worker**.
   a. Who was George Neele?
   b. How do we know about his life?

2. Read **Queen Victoria's train journeys**.
   a. What nearly happened at Forfar?
   b. Why was the Queen unhappy at Wigan and Oxford?

3. Would you trust what George Neele tells us? Explain your answer.

2.14 LIVING IN INDUSTRIAL BRITAIN

The Industrial Revolution greatly changed the lives of working people in Britain.

It also changed the lives of the rich and their servants.

LADY CHARLOTTE GUEST

Lady Charlotte married John Guest in 1833. She was 21 and he was 48. They had ten children.

John Guest was the owner of the Dowlais ironworks in South Wales. He made a lot of money from selling his iron. He died in 1852.

Lady Charlotte kept a diary. It tells us that she took an interest in the ironworks and politics. She also liked going to parties.

She helped the poor and set up a school in Dowlais for the workers' children.

Here are some extracts from her diary. The extracts are in *italics*.

Source A

Dowlais ironworks in South Wales.

Lady Charlotte and the railways

Lady Charlotte and John Guest did a lot of travelling. They usually went by coach and horse, but they started to use the railway.

It took us one-and-a-half hours to do the 36-mile journey. It would have taken over four hours by coach and horse. The train is also much smoother.

In 1837 Lady Charlotte laid the foundation stone for the Taff Valley Railway.

I was given a small hammer to hit the stone into place. I said I would rather use a big wooden mallet. The workmen thought this was very funny.

Lady Charlotte did not always enjoy going by train.

I went some of the way home on the Great Western Railway. The carriages rocked about like a steamship.

Lady Charlotte and factories

Lady Charlotte often visited factories. She was interested to see how things were made.

4 November 1833: Mr Houldsworth kindly showed us around his cotton factory.

I was most impressed by all the machinery. We even saw velvet embroidered by machine.

We then went to another factory and watched them making a steam coach. Once again there was all sorts of machinery.

Lady Charlotte and cholera

Cholera came to Dowlais in 1849.

31 May: The cholera has broken out in Cardiff. It could arrive in Dowlais soon. John has been to a meeting about cleaning the town. Houses are to be whitewashed.

9 June: Cholera has spread to the village across the river.

11 June: The first case of cholera has been reported in Dowlais. People are very frightened of catching it.

22 June: Cholera is all over Dowlais. Thirteen people are dying every day. I have sent for more doctors.

31 July: Twenty people are dying every day in Dowlais. I have moved out to the countryside with the children.

Lady Charlotte giving prizes at Dowlais school in about 1855.

Source B

Questions

1. Read **Lady Charlotte Guest**. Who was Lady Charlotte?
2. Even though she was rich, Lady Charlotte took an interest in working people. Do you agree?
3. How much can we learn from Lady Charlotte's diaries about life at the time?

Domestic servants

In the late 1800s over one million people worked as domestic servants.

Unlike factories and mines, there were no rules about the working conditions of servants. Some girls were just young children when they went to work as servants. The work was hard and the hours were long.

But by 1900 things were beginning to change. Read on.

HARRIET BROWN

Harriet Brown became a servant in 1870. She wrote home, telling her mother how hard it was.

I get up at 6.00 in the morning and do not get to bed until midnight. I work all day doing the fires and other jobs. Sometimes I feel so tired that I have a good cry. Mrs Graves, the cook, is kind to me. She helps me with my work, otherwise I would not get it all done.

What jobs did servants do?

Rich people who lived in big houses had lots of servants.

The servants lived in their own part of the house.

The most important servants were the butler and the lady's maid. They served the gentleman and lady of the house.

Some servants worked as gardeners or in the stables.

There were cooks, housemaids to dust, and scullery maids to work in the kitchen.

Some families could only afford one servant. They employed a local girl who lived in her own home. She came in each day to clean and cook.

Source C

The male servants at Petworth House in Sussex in the 1870s.

Source D

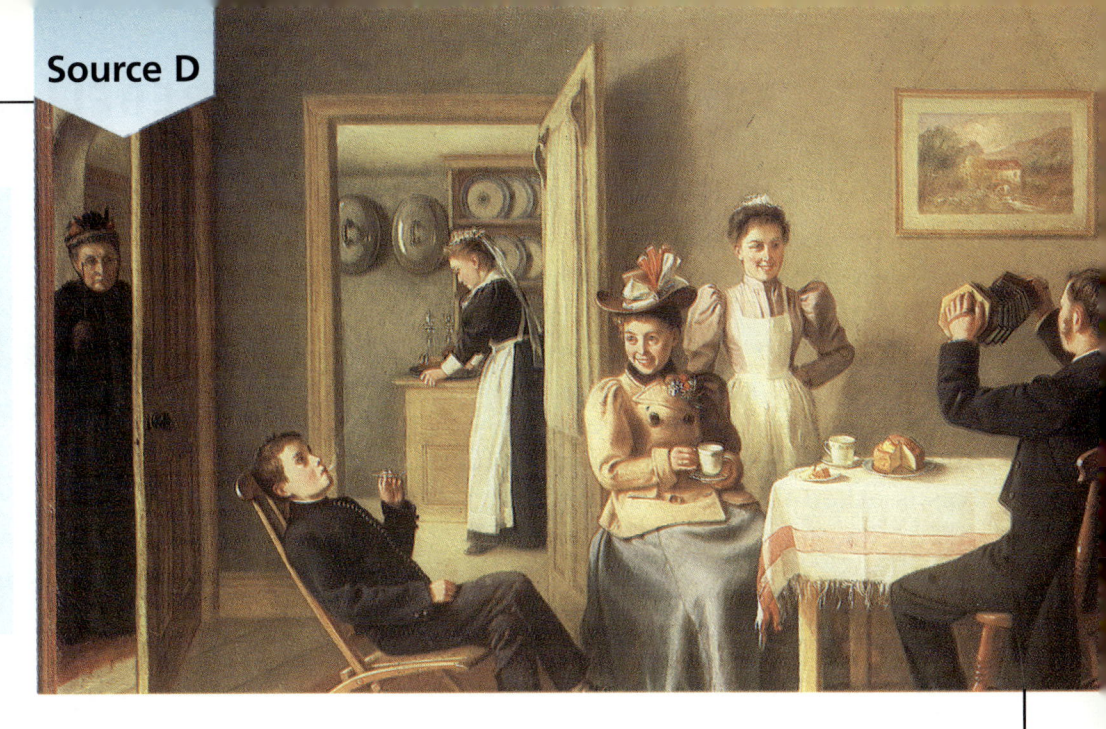

A former servant has come back to visit her old mistress. They are having a cup of tea and some fun.

Changes by 1900

New household machines, such as gas cookers, sewing machines and washing machines, came into use. This made life easier for servants.

Servants began to get more time off. They could visit the music hall or go on a railway outing to the seaside.

The Industrial Revolution brought a bigger choice of jobs. New inventions, such as typewriters and telephones, came into use.

Young women could now work as secretaries in an office or at a telephone exchange.

These jobs were more interesting and better paid than being a servant.

WILLIAM LANCERLY

I became a servant when I was sixteen. I cleaned shoes, sharpened knives, cleaned the silver and waited on people who came to dinner. I was then made a footman. After four years of service I was given some holiday!

I went to London and got a better job. My duties were easier and I was sometimes given an evening off to go to the theatre.

When I later had to employ servants myself, I found that servants' children were best. They were used to working hard and getting up early.

Questions

1 Read **Domestic servants**.
   How many people worked as servants?

2 Read **Harriet Brown**.
   What was it like to be a servant?

3 Read **Changes by 1900**.
   a Why did servants' jobs get easier?
   b What did they do when they had time off?
   c Why did fewer young women become servants?

3.1 WARS, RIOTS AND REBELLIONS

The American Revolution

Britain owned thirteen colonies in America. The Americans grew tired of being bossed about by Britain. In 1775 they rebelled against British rule. In 1776 the Americans wrote their Declaration of Independence. It said that all people should be free and equal. By 1783 the British had been thrown out of America. This is called the American Revolution.

Source A

The French Revolution

The poor people in France heard what the Americans had done. They liked the idea of being free and equal.

The French king was unpopular. The poor had to pay heavy taxes, but did not get a say in the government. The rich hardly paid any taxes at all.

In 1789 the poor rebelled. The king was thrown out of power. Things then got out of control and, in 1793, the king was executed. These events are called the French Revolution.

Monarchy (Louis XVI)	Revolutionary Government	Emperor Napoleon	Monarchy restored	Republic
1792	1794	1804	1830 1848	1849

The government of France, 1792–1849.

Source B

A cartoon from the 1790s. It shows what the French Revolution meant to other countries.

Europe is frightened

Ordinary people in other countries saw what had happened in France. They saw it was possible to throw bad rulers out of power.

'Copy-cat' revolutions took place in other countries in Europe. Most of them were put down. But governments were still very worried.

As for Britain?

The government was nervous that there might be a revolution in Britain. It quickly put down any hint of trouble from the workers. Here are two examples:

1 In 1819 a peaceful meeting was held at St Peter's Fields in Manchester. The crowd included women and children. They gathered to hear a speech about why working people should have the vote. The magistrates ordered soldiers to charge the crowd. Eleven people were killed and over four hundred were injured.

2 In 1834 six farm workers from Tolpuddle in Dorset formed a trade union to get higher wages. They were arrested and transported to Australia for seven years (see page 24).

There was never any chance of a revolution happening in Britain.

Questions

1 Read **The American Revolution**. What did the Americans do in 1775?

2 Read **The French Revolution**. What did the poor people of France do in 1789?

3 Read **As for Britain?** Why did Britain not have a revolution?

3.2 THE AMERICAN REVOLUTION

British colonies in America

Britain owned thirteen colonies in America (see map).

The colonies were separate from each other. They each had their own local parliament and laws.

But in the 1770s the colonies joined together to throw Britain out of America. They were tired of British rule.

Why did the American colonies fall out with Britain?

1 **The war with France.** The French also owned land in America. The British were frightened that they would lose land to the French. So, in 1756, the two countries went to war. The war was fought in America. The colonists helped Britain to beat the French. But Britain did not thank the American colonists for their help.

2 **Rules about trade.** Goods going in and out of America had to be carried on British ships. This made the colonists angry. They often dodged the rule by smuggling.

3 **Heavy taxes.** In 1765 Britain brought in the Stamp Act. This said that the colonists had to pay a tax on newspapers and legal documents. The tax was to pay for the British army in America. The colonists refused to pay the tax.

4 **The Boston Massacre, 1770.** The British still put taxes on goods going into America. The colonists were angry. In 1770 there was a riot in Boston. British soldiers fired on the crowd and five people were killed.

5 **The Boston Tea Party.** In 1773 a cargo of tea came into the port of Boston. The colonists raided the ships and dumped 340 chests of tea into the harbour. They were protesting about having to pay tax on it. The British closed the port and sent in soldiers to keep order.

The thirteen British colonies in 1775.

The Battle of Princetown, 1777. The British are in red coats. The man on the white horse is George Washington. He became the first President of the USA.

The War of American Independence, 1775–83

The quarrel became so bad that war broke out between Britain and the colonists.

In 1775 British soldiers in Boston decided to march on the town of Concord. This was where the colonists kept their weapons. A message was sent to Concord, warning the people that the British were coming. On their way back from Concord the British were attacked by the colonists at Lexington. War had started.

Declaration of Independence

On 4 July 1776 the Americans published the Declaration of Independence. It was written by Thomas Jefferson. It said that all men should be free and equal.

The British are beaten

Everyone thought that Britain would win the war easily but they were wrong.

France and Spain helped the Americans.

By 1781 the British were beaten. They surrendered at Yorktown.

A peace treaty was made in 1783. Britain agreed that the American colonies could have their independence.

Becoming an American

Now the colonists were free of Britain, they needed to work out how to govern themselves. This was done by the American Congress (parliament). It said that:

- The colonies would become **states**. Each state would have its own government for local matters.

- Each state would be a part of the United States of America.

Questions

1 Read **Declaration of Independence**.
   a Who wrote the American Declaration of Independence?
   b When was it published?

2 Read page 74. Why did the Americans fall out with the British?

Paul Revere – hero of the American Revolution?

Paul Revere the rebel

Paul Revere lived in Boston. He was a silversmith and an engraver. Revere hated the British and took part in the **Boston Tea Party**. He wrote leaflets against the British. Revere was also a messenger who went around telling people how bad the British were.

Paul Revere's midnight ride

The British army was going to march from Boston to Lexington and then to Concord. At Concord they were going to destroy the guns the Americans had hidden there.

At 10.00 pm on 18 April 1775, Revere was told to ride to Concord to tell people that the British were coming. He rode hard, warning people along the way. William Dawes, a second messenger, was sent a different way.

Revere arrived in Lexington at midnight. He met up with Dawes. They were joined by Dr Samuel Prescott, who had been visiting his girlfriend in Lexington. Prescott had never done anything before against the British. The three men set off for Concord.

Arrested

Along the road they were arrested by a British patrol. Dawes escaped back to Lexington, but Revere was held prisoner. He was later released and walked back to Lexington. Prescott escaped. His horse jumped a fence and he rode to Concord to tell the people that the British were coming.

Henry Longfellow

In 1860 Henry Longfellow wrote a poem called *Paul Revere's Ride* (see page 77). It tells how Revere rode to warn people that the British were coming. The poem makes Revere look like a hero. It does not even mention Prescott and says that Revere reached Concord!

Source B

Even after the American Revolution, fighting continued between the British and the Americans, mainly at sea. This picture, painted in 1815, shows one such fight.

Part of *Paul Revere's Ride*, by Henry Wadsworth Longfellow.

*Listen my children and you shall hear
Of the midnight ride of Paul Revere,
On the eighteenth of April in Seventy-five;
Hardly a man is now alive
Who remembers that famous day and year.*

*It was twelve by the village clock,
When he crossed the bridge into Medford town
He heard the crowing of the cock,
And the barking of the farmer's dog,
And felt the damp of the river fog,
That rises after the sun goes down.*

*It was one by the village clock
When he galloped into Lexington.
He saw the gilded weathercock
Swim in the moonlight as he passed.*

*It was two by the village clock
When he came to the bridge in Concord town.
He heard the bleating of the flock,
And the twitter of birds among the trees
And felt the breath of the morning breeze
Blowing over the meadows brown.*

*So through the night rode Paul Revere;
And so through the night went his cry of alarm.*

Source C

Paul Revere's ride was still being sung about in 1900.

Questions

1 Read **Paul Revere's midnight ride**.
   a What were Revere and William Dawes told to do?
   b Who was Samuel Prescott?

2 Read **Arrested**.
   Which of the three men reached Concord?

3 Read **Henry Longfellow** and the poem on this page.
   a Does this poem tell the full story?
   b Do you think Revere really was a hero or has history made him a hero?

3.3 THE GIFT OF LIBERTY

Source A

The Statue of Liberty

The Statue of Liberty is at the entrance to New York Harbour. In her left hand is a torch. In her right hand is a stone with the date 4 July 1776 carved on it. This was the date when America declared its independence from Britain.

Source B

From the *American Declaration of Independence*, 1776.

All men are equal. Everyone has the right to freedom and happiness.

The head of the Statue of Liberty in an exhibition in Paris.

The American Civil War, 1861–5

Black people also wanted liberty. The Civil War was about whether or not to end slavery and make black people in America free. It was fought between the northern states and the southern states.

The north wanted to end slavery; the south wanted to keep slavery.

The north won. Slavery in the USA came to an end. Lots of black slaves got their freedom.

A gift from France

France gave the Statue of Liberty to America in 1886. Why?

1 To celebrate black slaves getting their freedom after the Civil War.
2 The Americans rebelled against Britain in 1776 and won. This gave the French people the idea to rebel against their king in 1789. The statue was a reminder of this.
3 Giving a statue would make France look generous.

America – the land of hope?

At the bottom of the statue it says that America is a country which will take in and help poor people from other countries.

During the 1800s thousands of people went to America from Europe, hoping to start a new and better life.

But by the 1890s the Americans were worried that too many **immigrants** were arriving. So they made it harder for people to get into America.

Anyone who was ill or disabled was sent back. In the 1920s America would only let a certain number of people into the country.

Source C

On 4 July 1852, a free black man was asked to make a speech to celebrate America's independence. This is what he said.

The 4 July 1776 means nothing to black people. The date belongs to white people.

There are thousands of black people still living in slavery in America. They are in chains. They have nothing to celebrate.

Questions

1 Read **Source B**. What did the *Declaration of Independence* say?

2 Read **The Statue of Liberty**.
  a What is the lady holding in her right hand?
  b Why do you think this is?

3 Read **A gift from France**. Why did France give America the Statue of Liberty?

4 Read **Source C**.
  a Why was this man still angry?
  b Look at this page. When were black slaves freed?

3.4 THE FRENCH REVOLUTION

Why did the French Revolution break out?

In 1789 rioting against King Louis XVI broke out in Paris. The French Revolution of 1789 had started. Why did this happen?

1. France was divided into three **estates** (groups). These were:
   - The First Estate (bishops and priests).
   - The Second Estate (nobles).
   - The Third Estate (the middle class and peasants).

   The Third Estate had no say in the government, yet they had to pay the most taxes. Church people and nobles hardly paid any taxes at all. It was very unfair.

2. The king ran France on his own. Parliament had not met since 1614. France was badly run. The peasants were fed up with this.

3. In 1788 there was a bad harvest. The price of bread shot up. The peasants could not afford to buy it. Many peasants went to Paris to complain.

ROBESPIERRE

Robespierre ran the government after King Louis XVI had been thrown out of power.

Robespierre was frightened of losing power himself. So he ordered lots of people to be executed by the guillotine. Most of them had done nothing wrong. People called it 'The Terror'.

In 1794 Robespierre was executed by his enemies.

The storming of the Bastille prison, 14 July 1789.

Source A

Parliament is called

By 1789 the king had run out of money. He wanted to raise more taxes. He could only do this by calling Parliament. When Parliament met it asked for a say in running the country. The king refused. The cartoon shows what happened next.

Source B

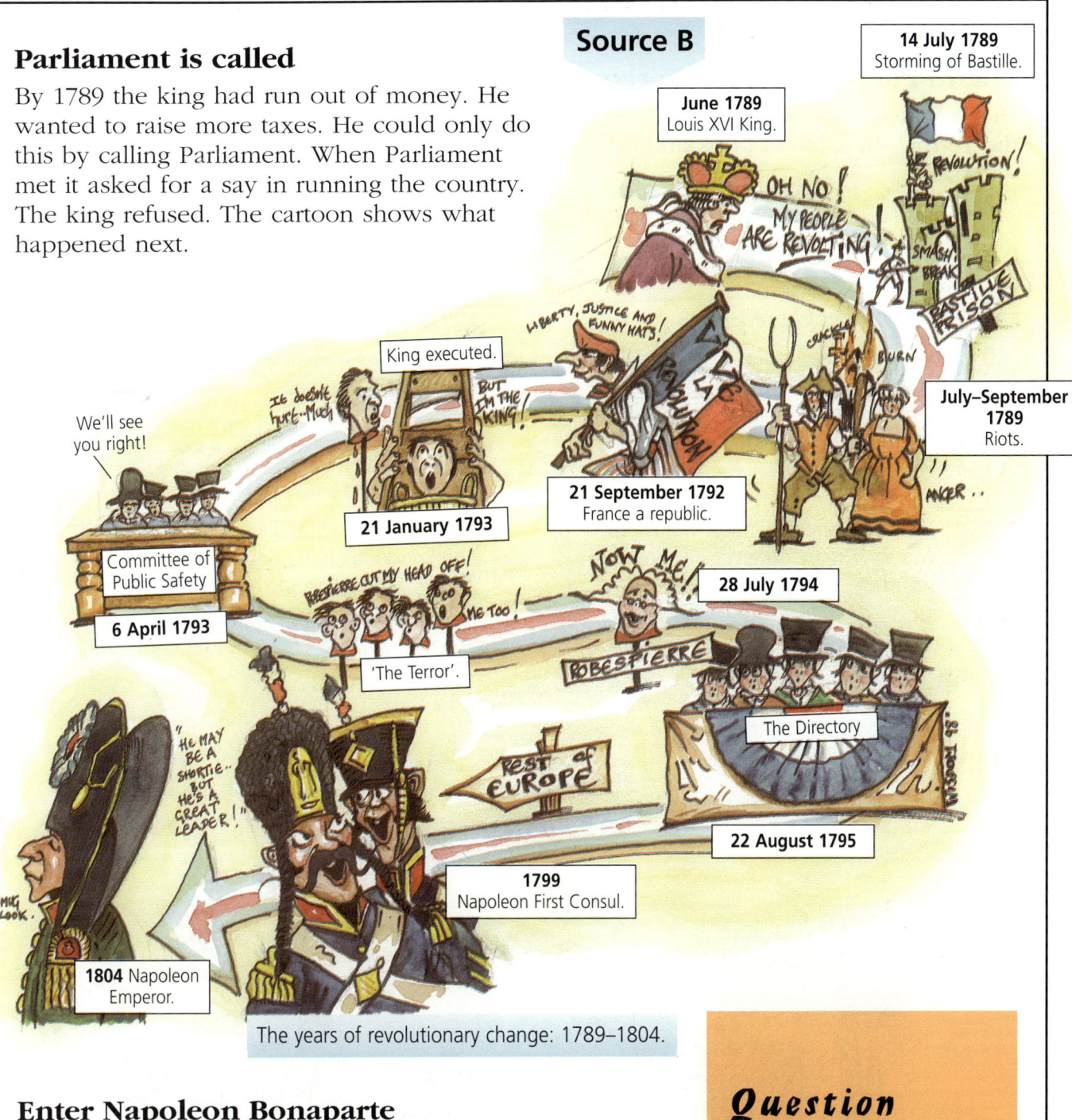

The years of revolutionary change: 1789–1804.

Enter Napoleon Bonaparte

Napoleon Bonaparte rose to power quickly after 1793. By 1799 he was the most powerful man in France. By 1804 he was the Emperor of France. You can read about him on pages 84–7.

Question

Read **Why did the French Revolution break out?** Write a paragraph in your own words saying why the people rebelled against Louis XVI.

Life in Paris during the Terror

Helen Williams was English. She lived in Paris during the Terror. She wrote a book about it. Read on!

A nasty atmosphere

There was a nasty atmosphere in Paris. The king had been thrown out. The new government was very nervous. It thought that the king still had many followers. They were just waiting for the right moment to bring back the king.

Anyone could be arrested if they were suspected of plotting against the government. No proof was needed!

Everyone had to be careful – even priests and bankers!

The government sent round soldiers to make sure its new laws were being obeyed.

Prison

The government said foreigners were safe and would not be harmed.

Then things changed. A lot of our friends were arrested.

We were woken in the middle of the night by a loud knocking on the door. Two government soldiers were waiting to arrest us. We were thrown into prison.

An English cartoon from 1792. It shows supporters of the Revolution cooking and eating people!

Source C

WHO WAS HELEN WILLIAMS?

Helen Williams lived in Paris from 1788.

She liked the idea of people being free and equal.

Then the new government started arresting people for doing nothing. Helen was horrified.

She wrote to the newspapers in England. She told them that hundreds of people were going to the guillotine.

Helen was frightened for her life and went to Switzerland for a time.

Helen told the truth about all the executions. But she does not tell us about the good things done by the new government, such as the better schools and lower bread prices.

A nervous freedom

Luckily, my sister's French boyfriend got us out of prison. We were scared that we would be arrested again. There were spies everywhere. We jumped every time there was a knock on the door.

More and more people were having their heads chopped off by the guillotine. Some were arrested for being 'too clever'. Others for being 'too rich'. Some people were not given a reason.

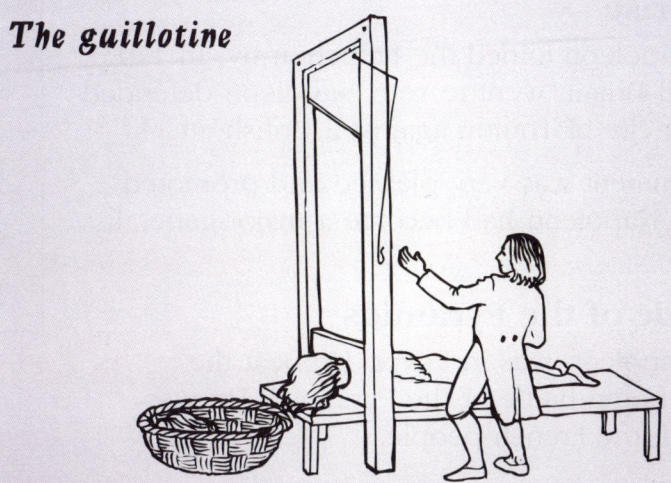

The guillotine

A guillotine.

Many went bravely to the guillotine. Others screamed loudly. The guillotine sliced off their heads. The gutters were streaming with blood.

The Terror gets worse

Robespierre was running the government at this time. Even his friends were not safe from arrest. People were very scared. There was nothing they could do to stop all the executions. Some people were so frightened that they committed suicide.

Questions

1. Read **Robespierre** on page 80.
   a. Who was Robespierre?
   b. What was the Terror?

2. Read **A nasty atmosphere** on page 82.
   Why were so many people being executed?

3. Read **Who was Helen Williams?**
   Would you trust what she tells us about life in Paris?

4. **Source C** was drawn in England in 1792. Would you trust what it shows?

3.5 NAPOLEON – EMPEROR OF FRANCE

Napoleon's early life
Napoleon Bonaparte was born in Corsica in 1769. His father was a lawyer. Napoleon went to train as a soldier in Paris. He was very clever. It only took him a year to pass the two-year course!

A rapid rise
In 1785 Napoleon joined the French army. In 1793 France and Britain went to war. Napoleon defended the French city of Toulon against a British attack.

The government was very pleased and promoted him. Soon Napoleon had become a major-general.

The Battle of the Pyramids
In 1798 Napoleon was in Egypt. He beat the Egyptians in the Battle of the Pyramids. He was a hero with the French people.

Napoleon takes control
Napoleon went back to Paris. The government had become unpopular. Napoleon had the army on his side and in 1799 he took control of the government.

He was called the First Consul.

Popularity
Many French people were pleased that Napoleon was in control. They thought he would be a strong leader.

In 1804 Napoleon crowned himself the Emperor of France.

Source A
Until 1768 Corsica was owned by Italy.

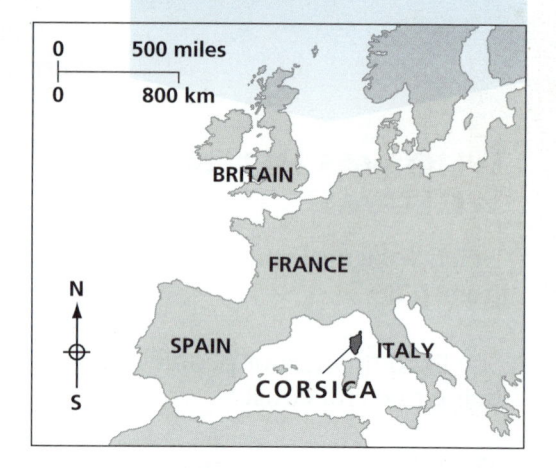

Napoleon had lots of illnesses!

- Constipation and **piles**
- Pain when urinating
- Scars and pain from old battle wounds
- A disease which caused shrinking of the penis
- Stomach cancer (which eventually killed him)

Source B

Napoleon's coronation, painted by Jacques Louis David. Napoleon is shown crowning himself. David was Napoleon's chief artist.

Napoleon's bad points as a ruler

Napoleon said he supported the Revolution. He said that he believed in freedom and people being equal. But some of his changes went against this:

- He made himself the Emperor, even though the Revolution had done away with the king.
- He allowed nobles, even though the Revolution had banned them.
- There were no elections when he became Emperor. So people were not free to choose the government!
- He would not let the newspapers say what they wanted. This went against freedom.
- He set up a secret police force to spy on his enemies in France.

Questions

1. Read **Napoleon takes control**.
   a. When did Napoleon take control of the government?
   b. Why was he able to do this?
   c. What did he do in 1804?

2. Read **Napoleon's good points as ruler**.
   What did he do to make things better?

3. Look at the cartoon on page 84.
   Even though he was very powerful, Napoleon was not healthy. What illnesses did he have?

Napoleon's good points as a ruler

Napoleon did bring in some good changes in France.

- He brought in the Code Napoleon, a set of laws. The Code said that the poor should be treated the same as everyone else.
- He made the schools better.
- He spent a lot of money on grand new buildings in Paris.

85

Napoleon the soldier

Napoleon beats Austria

When Napoleon became a general, France was at war with Austria, Britain and Russia. He beat the Austrians at the Battle of Marengo in 1800. A peace treaty was made which gave France a lot of land in Europe.

Now for Britain!

Napoleon was tired of Britain making trouble for him. So in 1804 he decided to invade Britain.

Napoleon needed a strong navy to protect his soldiers as they crossed the English Channel.

But, in 1805, Lord Nelson destroyed the French navy at the Battle of Trafalgar. Napoleon called off the invasion of Britain.

Source C

By 1810 Napoleon ruled most of Europe. It seemed that no one could stop him.

Source D

Napoleon running away from the battlefield at Waterloo.

Source E

Said by a Russian about the French as they left Moscow.

I saw a dead man inside a horse. He had cut away its stomach so he could keep warm.

The French soldiers were so hungry, they were eating the flesh of dead bodies.

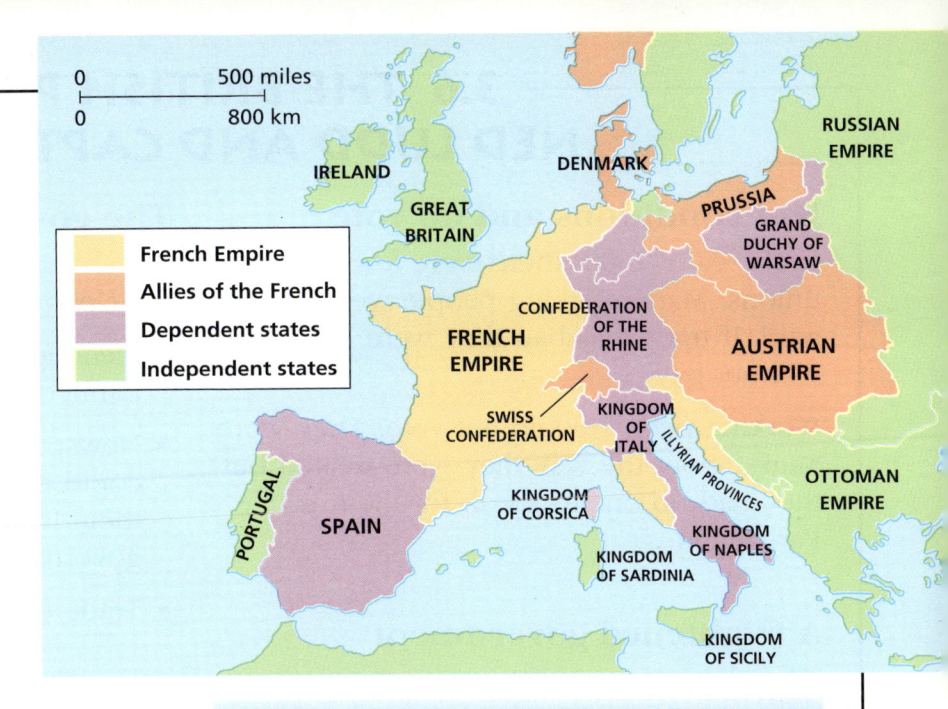

Europe in 1810.

Napoleon in control

Napoleon won a lot of battles after 1805. By 1810 he ruled most of Europe (look at the map). He would not allow countries under his control to trade with Britain.

Things go wrong

In 1808 the king of Spain died. Napoleon told the Spanish that his brother would be the new king. The Spanish did not want this.

Napoleon invaded Spain. Britain sent the Duke of Wellington to help the Spanish. By 1813 Napoleon's soldiers had been driven back into France.

A big mistake

In 1812 Napoleon invaded Russia. The Russians burned the crops as they retreated, leaving no food for the French soldiers.

When the French reached Moscow the cold winter set in. It forced Napoleon to pull out of Russia. Thousands of soldiers died on their way back to France. Out of an army of 600,000 men, only 50,000 made it back.

The Battle of Waterloo, 1815

In 1814 Napoleon surrendered. He was banished to the island of Elba. But he escaped and made his way back to France.

Napoleon raised an army, but was finally beaten at the Battle of Waterloo.

This time he was sent much further away to St Helena. He died there in 1821.

Question

Read **The Battle of Waterloo, 1815**. St Helena is 8,000 kilometres from France. Why do you think Napoleon was sent so far away?

3.6 THE BRITISH PROTEST: NED LUDD AND CAPTAIN SWING

Bad conditions and no vote

In the early 1800s there were few trade unions. Many working people were badly paid. If trade was bad they were laid off without pay.

Working people could not vote. They were angry about the way they were treated but they had no one to speak for them in Parliament.

A frightened government

The government was frightened. It wanted poor people kept in their place. Otherwise they might start a revolution like the French in 1789.

Source A

William Horsfall, a Yorkshire mill owner, was shot dead by Luddites in 1812.

Horsfall had publicly criticised the Luddites and so they decided to shoot him. Three Luddites were hanged for his murder.

The government clamps down

Laws were passed to keep the workers in their place.

- Meetings of over fifty people were banned.
- Newspapers were taxed so the workers could not afford them. This stopped them from reading criticisms of the government.
- Trade unions were banned.

The Luddites, 1811–12

Many workers were worried that the new machines which were invented during the Industrial Revolution would put them out of work. During 1811 and 1812 workers smashed up many machines with huge hammers. They also burned down the factories. Often the workers sent a warning (see Source B).

Source B

A Luddite warning, 1812.

To Mr Smith of Huddersfield

Sir

I have found out that you have one of those hateful new machines. If you do not remove it I will send 300 men to smash it up.

They will then burn down your factory. If you shoot at my men, they have orders to kill you.

Signed

General Ned Ludd

Source C

The Home of the Rick Burner, a cartoon from Punch magazine, 1844.

Source D

A 'Swing' letter, threatening to burn down a school. The owner must have been a supporter of the threshing machines.

The warning letters were always signed by a 'Ned Ludd'. The Luddites were named after him. No one knows for sure if there was such a person as Ned Ludd.

The government passed a law which said that people would be hanged if they were caught smashing machines.

The Swing Riots, 1830

Threshing corn had always been done by hand. It provided winter jobs for the farm workers.

By 1830 many farmers had bought threshing machines. They could do the work of many men.

Farm labourers in the south and east were thrown out of work. Many labourers and their families were starving because they had no money coming in.

In 1830 rioting broke out. Haystacks were burned down and threshing machines were smashed up. The riots started in Kent and soon spread across the south of England.

Often the farmers were sent threatening letters. They were signed by a 'Captain Swing'. No one knows for sure whether he was a real person or not.

The government punished the rioters. Nineteen labourers were hanged, 481 were transported to Australia and 644 were sent to prison.

Questions

1. Read **A frightened government**. Why was the government so frightened of the workers?

2. Read **The Luddites, 1811–12**. What did the Luddites do and why?

3. Read **The Swing Riots, 1830**.
   a. What did the Swing rioters do and why?
   b. What did the government do to punish the rioters and why?

4. Did the Luddites and Swing Rioters achieve anything in the end?

3.7 THE BRITISH PROTEST: REBECCA

Hard times in Wales

Life was hard for people in west Wales. Wages were low and many working people were hungry. The farmers had also hit hard times. Their crops and animals were fetching low prices at market.

People could not afford to pay tolls to travel on the new turnpike roads. Farmers were even charged to take their animals along the turnpike roads. People were angry. They could take no more.

Riots break out, 1839

On 6 June 1839 a gang of men led by Tom Rees (see box) went to the toll gates at Efailwen carrying hammers, axes and torches. They had blackened faces and wore women's clothes. The gang smashed down the tollgates and burned down the toll-keeper's house.

Lots of other attacks on tollgates took place. The leader was always called Rebecca. No one really knows why. Some say it was after a woman in the Bible. Others say it was because Tom Rees had borrowed his clothes from a woman called Rebecca.

TOM REES (1806–76)

Tom was a farm worker. He was married with three children. He read the Bible a lot.

Tom was a boxer in his spare time. He had bruises and scars all over his body. In one fight he lost an eye!

Source A

This was said by the leader before a gate was smashed down.

My children, something is in the way.

Source B

Rebecca and Her Daughters, painted in the nineteenth century.

Was there just one 'Rebecca'?

Many believed that there were lots of different leaders and they all copied the name of 'Rebecca'.

Others thought that there was only one 'Rebecca' and he was Hugh Williams in disguise.

Hugh Williams was a farmer and lawyer who defended rioters in court. He told a friend that he was the leader of the riots.

Source C

From a letter sent to a newspaper in 1843.

The people are with me. They are all my followers. Their lives are hard and this is why they follow me.

I see coal men dressed in rags and farmers' wives carrying heavy baskets to market. I see farm workers having to live on barley bread and skimmed milk.

I know they are all my daughters [followers].

A picture of Rebecca, drawn at the time.

Source D

Riots again

The rioting started again in 1842. Tollgates were smashed down all over west Wales.

Soldiers were called in to deal with the riots. Two leaders were captured and taken to court. They laughed when they were sentenced to transportation!

Questions

1 Read **Hard times in Wales**.
   a Why was life hard?
   b Why were people angry about tollgates being set up?

2 Read **Riots break out, 1839**.
   a What happened on 6 June 1839?
   b What was the leader always called?
   c Why was this so?

3.8 THE BRITISH PROTEST: THE CHARTISTS

The People's Charter

Working people lived very hard lives in the early 1800s. They were not allowed to vote. So they had no one to speak for them in Parliament. Most MPs in Parliament were rich landowners and farmers.

The People's Charter (see Source A) came out in 1838. People who supported it were called Chartists.

The Chartists wanted working people to be able to vote. Then they could have MPs who would speak out for them. The Chartists said this was the only way to make things better.

What did the Chartists do?

In 1839 the Chartists took a **petition** to Parliament. It had one million signatures. The petition asked for the Charter to be passed by Parliament. But Parliament threw it out.

Source A

The People's Charter:

1 A vote for every man over 21.

2 Secret voting.

3 People should not have to own land to be an MP.

4 MPs should be paid.

5 Equal voting districts.

6 An election every year.

In 1839, 1842 and 1848 the Chartists sent petitions to Parliament, asking for the Charter to be allowed. Each time Parliament threw the petition out. This picture shows the second petition being taken to Parliament in 1842. It had three million signatures.

Source B

Violence

After this John Frost led a group of armed miners into Newport to free some Chartists from prison. There was a battle with soldiers and 24 men were killed.

In 1842 a second petition was sent to Parliament. It was turned down again. There were riots in the north of England. Soldiers were sent to restore order.

One last try

In 1848 the Chartists drew up a third petition. It had six million signatures. When Parliament looked at the petition many signatures were forged. It had names like 'Flat nose' and 'Pug nose' on it. Parliament threw it out. Chartism was finished.

Source C

The two main leaders of the Chartists were Feargus O'Connor and William Lovett.

If peaceful ways do not work, we must use force and violence.

(Feargus O'Connor)

Guns are no good. We must argue peacefully.

(William Lovett)

Source D

One of the first photographs ever taken. It shows a big Chartist meeting in London in 1848.

Questions

1. Read **Source A**.
   What did the Chartists want?

2. Read **The People's Charter**.
   Why did people join the Chartists?

3. Read **Source C**.
   a Name two Chartist leaders.
   b How were their views different?

4. Read **One last try**.
   Why would Parliament not allow the Charter?

5. Look at **Source D**.
   Would you trust this photograph? Explain your answer.

3.9 MARTHA CARPENTER: A COUNTRY CHILDHOOD

Changes in the world
Martha Carpenter was born in 1849 and died in 1947. She lived through many changes.

Martha's family
Martha had an older brother and sister, and two brothers who died as babies. She was born in Datchworth in Hertfordshire on 7 August 1849. She was baptised in the parish church when she was one month old.

Working parents
Martha's father was called Edmund. Her mother was called Eliza. They worked for local farmers. They probably went to the hiring fairs in Hertford, the nearest town. All the farmers and farmworkers for miles around gathered at these fairs. The farmers offered jobs to the men and women they wanted. The jobs were all to do with running a farm.

Working on the farm
Edmund probably did jobs like digging ditches, mending fences and ploughing fields. Eliza may have worked in the fields too, particularly at harvest time. But she may have worked indoors on the farm doing jobs like making cheese and butter, baking bread and brewing ale.

Source A
Datchworth parish church. This is where Martha was baptised. Her parents and brothers and sister were buried here.

Source B
From the *Daily News*, 1891.

The country roads are crowded with wagons piled high with all the goods of farmworkers moving home. They have been to hiring fairs and are moving tables, chairs, beds and boxes to the new master's farm.

Questions
1. What sort of jobs would a farmworker like Edmund have done?
2. What sort of jobs would a farmworker like Eliza have done?
3. a How old was Martha when she started work?
   b What job did she do?
4. How did Martha better herself?

Source C

At harvest time the whole village turned out to help.

Source D

Tom Mullins was a farmworker. He was born in 1863. This is what he remembers.

A man could cut half an acre of corn a day and bind it into sheaves. Men worked in groups of twelve to twenty.

How country folk laughed when they saw the first machines. Some mowing machines were used as reapers, with a dozen men following behind binding the cut corn. Men were paid sixpence for a bundle of 24 sheaves.

When I was seventeen I earned £16 a year and my keep. Bread was three pence a quarter loaf, milk three pence a quart, tobacco three pence an ounce, while beer was two pence a pint, the best was three pence.

School or work?

Martha did not go to school. School was not free then, so her parents could not afford to send her. She started work in the fields when she was three or four years old. Her first job was scaring birds away from the corn. When she was older she worked weeding between rows and rows of vegetables. She was often hungry. One day she pulled up a turnip and ate it raw.

Working at the big house

When Martha was twelve she went to work in a rich person's house. There were many servants. She was a nursery maid and her job was to help the nanny and nurse to look after the children. The children also had a governess (their own teacher at home). Martha used the children's books to teach herself to read and write in the evenings after the children were asleep.

Off to London

Mr and Mrs Steel came to visit. They were rich people from London. Mrs Steel was impressed by Martha. She offered her a job as lady's maid. Martha packed everything she owned into a tin box and set off for London. She was eighteen years old.

3.10 MARTHA CARPENTER: GROWN-UP IN LONDON

Source A

This photograph was taken when Martha was a lady's maid. She borrowed Mrs Steel's dress so that she would look very smart.

Martha the lady's maid

Martha lived in the Steels' house in London. She worked as Mrs Steel's lady's maid. She looked after all her mistress's clothes, helped her do her hair and kept everything clean and tidy.

London in the 1860s and 1870s

London was an exciting place. There were horse-drawn cabs and carts delivering everything from beer to meat. The pavements were crowded with all sorts of people. There were flower sellers, pie sellers, beggars, crossing sweepers, ladies with their maids, nannies with children, businessmen and messenger boys, prostitutes and policemen. It was very different from the muddy lanes in the country.

Martha marries

Martha met George Crane and married him on Christmas Day 1876. Martha was 27 years old. George was 24 years old. Few employers allowed women to continue as servants when they married. Martha stopped being a lady's maid, though she may have done temporary work. Martha and George went to live with George's parents in Islington (another part of London).

Married life

George worked as a brewer's drayman. Martha was soon busy looking after a growing family. They had four children – three girls and a boy. Soon they moved to another house in Islington and took in lodgers. Later they ran a pub at the end of the road.

Questions

1 Look at **Source B**. When do you think the photograph was taken? Explain how you worked it out.

2 Write about the ways in which life changed during Martha's lifetime.

Source B

Martha with two of her daughters.

The family grows up

All the children went to school. When the girls left they trained to make clothes. They were each given a sewing machine for their 21st birthday. Their brother, Henry, had tuberculosis and died in 1900 when he was 20 years old. Martha and George stayed in Islington until George died in 1928.

Changes in Martha's life

Martha lived until she was 98.

She grew up in a time when most jobs were done by hand or heavy work was done by horses.

She never went to school but taught herself to read. She came from a poor family but bettered herself by working for rich people. Then she married and brought up a family.

By the time Martha died, there were cars, aeroplanes, films, radio, television, telephones or electricity. In fact, all these things were very common.

Source C

Martha aged 96 years old. She was living with her daughter in Northampton.

THE MODERN WORLD: AN INTRODUCTION

Empires counted

The twentieth century has been a time of change. As the maps on these two pages show, the world in the 1990s is very different from the world in 1900. The European powers no longer have empires with lots of colonies.

World powers in 1900

The richest and most important powers in 1900 were Britain, Russia, France, the USA, Germany, Austria-Hungary, Italy and Japan.

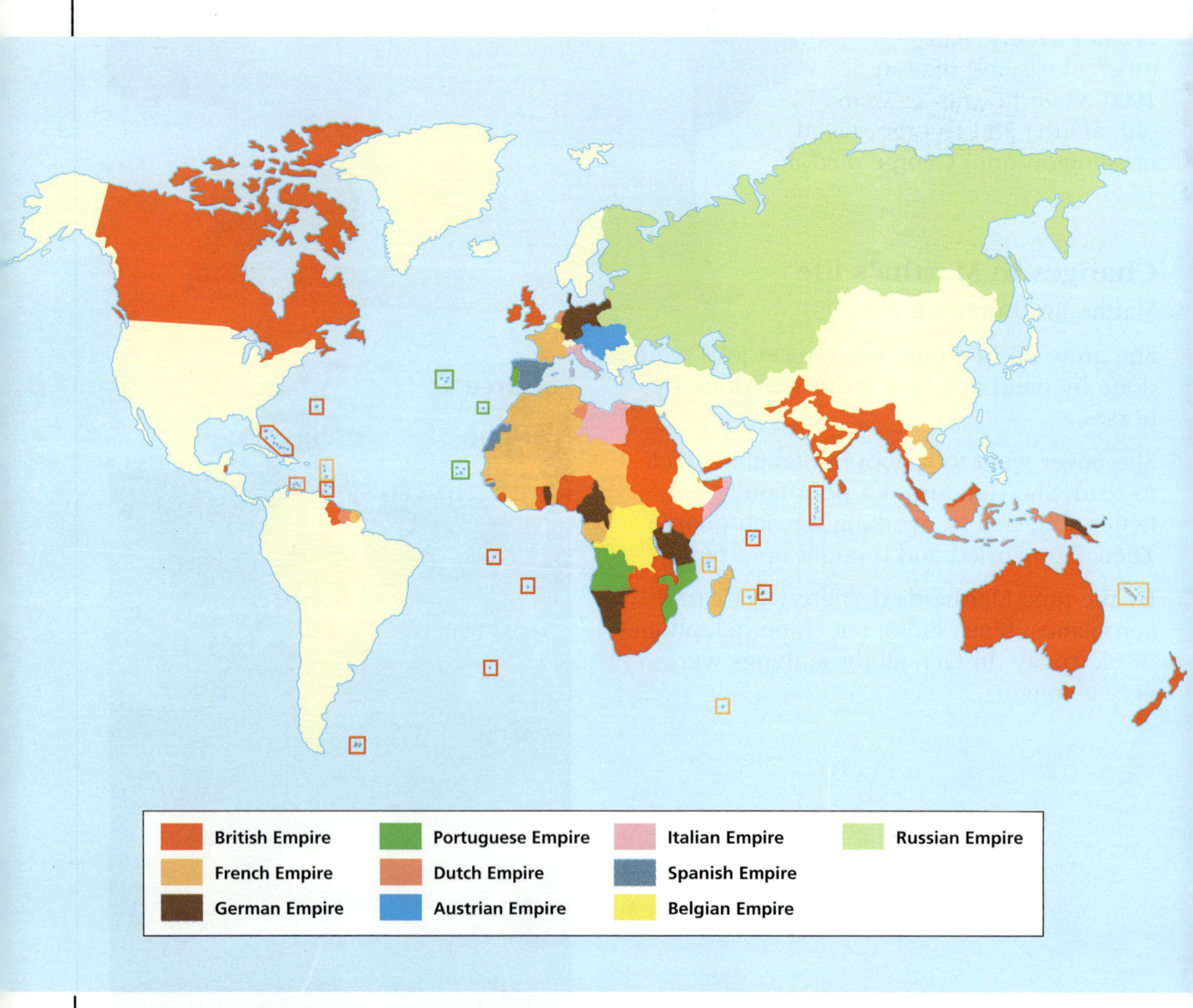

- British Empire
- French Empire
- German Empire
- Portuguese Empire
- Dutch Empire
- Austrian Empire
- Italian Empire
- Spanish Empire
- Belgian Empire
- Russian Empire

The world in 1900.

Wealth counts

In the 1990s, the power of a country is measured by how strong a force it is in world affairs. This really means how rich it is. The USA is one of the strongest forces in the world. It is also the richest.

World powers in the 1990s

The richest countries in the 1990s are the USA, Germany, Japan, France, Italy, Britain, Switzerland, Finland, Luxembourg and the United Arab Emirates.

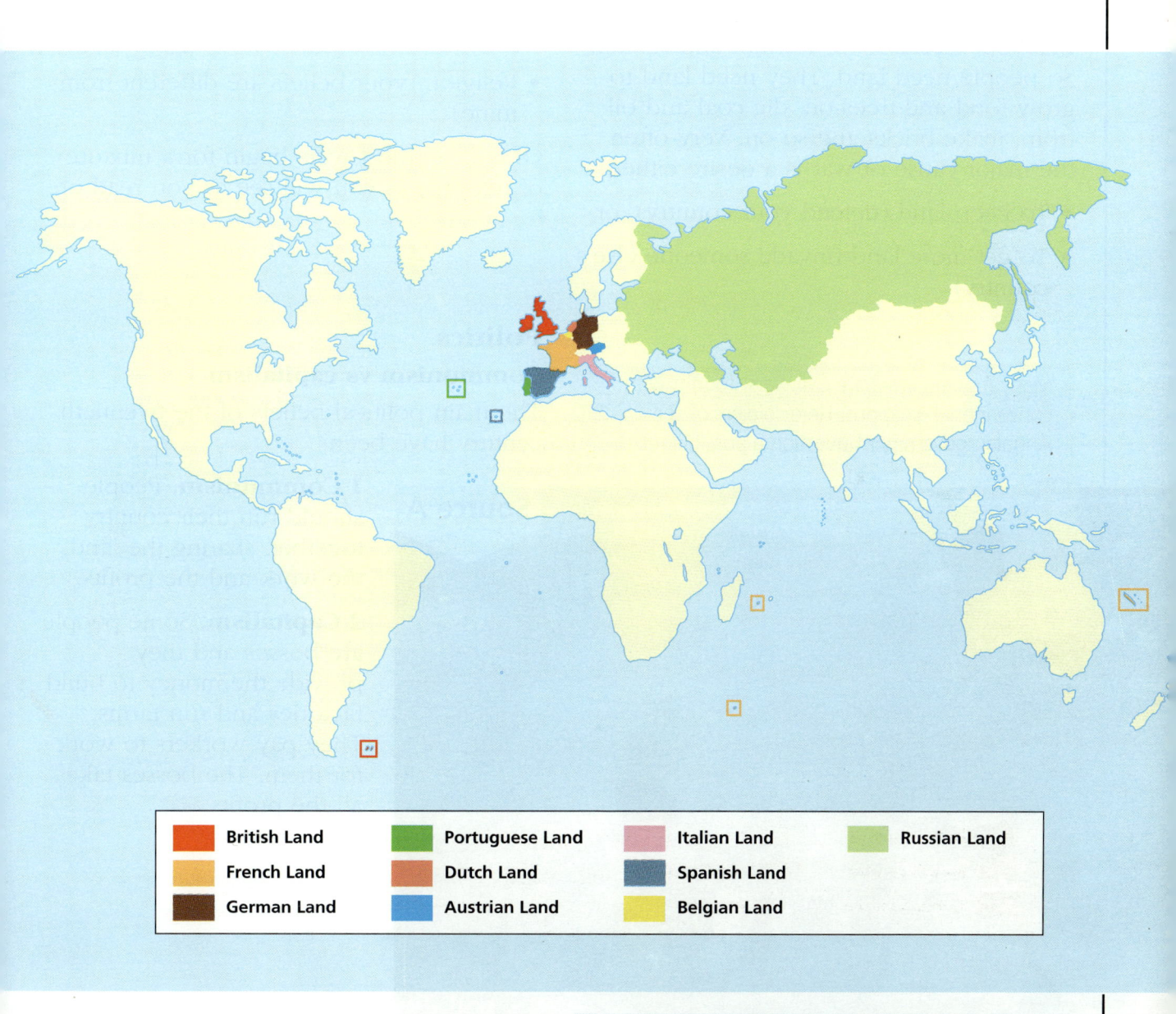

■ British Land	■ Portuguese Land	■ Italian Land	■ Russian Land
■ French Land	■ Dutch Land	■ Spanish Land	
■ German Land	■ Austrian Land	■ Belgian Land	

The world in 1997.

99

War in the twentieth century

There have been two major world wars:

- The First World War, 1914–18.
- The Second World War, 1939–45.

Most years since 1900 have seen wars somewhere in the world.

What leads to war?

Everyone needs food, warmth and shelter. So people need land. They need land to grow food and trees on, dig coal and oil from, make bricks and so on. Very often the major cause of war is a desire either:

- To keep land (defend your country), or
- To get more land (invade someone else's country).

Many modern wars are civil wars, fought with conventional weapons. Here soldiers of the Angolan government question a possible rebel.

Source A

Other reasons

But there are many other reasons for war. These are often to do with people or countries feeling threatened and frightened. These reasons may be:

- Politics (you run your country differently from mine).
- Trade (I do not want you to stop me trading with other countries and making money).
- Religion (your beliefs are different from mine).

Of course, most wars begin for a mixture of reasons, as you will see as you read on.

Politics

Communism vs capitalism

The main political beliefs of the twentieth century have been:

1 Communism. People should run their country together, sharing the land, the work and the profits.

2 Capitalism. Some people are bosses and they provide the money to build factories and run farms. They pay workers to work for them. The bosses take all the profits.

The Cold War

The USSR was a communist country. The USA was a capitalist country. Each of them was afraid of the other. They were afraid they might be conquered and have to change the way they ran their country. In 1991 the USSR gave up communism. The only major power still governed by communism is China.

A shrinking world

In the 1900s there were still areas of the world unexplored. Nowadays there are satellites in space, which means that people can communicate with places on the other side of the world instantly. In 1969 the first men landed on the moon. There are now other space explorations too.

A healthier world?

Medical discoveries have helped to fight disease all over the world. Diseases such as smallpox and leprosy have either disappeared or can be treated. But there is still a long way to go. More than half the world's children do not have enough food to eat. There are still many places that do not have clean water supplies. There are many places where people cannot afford to buy a simple pain killer like aspirin.

Source B

1900–98

World population

1900	1998
160,000,000	5,925,770,871

Average life expectancy

1900	1998
Men 45	Men 73
Women 48	Women 79

Life expectancy, 1998

Republic of San Marino (highest)
(developed country)   85
Rwanda (lowest)
(in Third World)   36

Question

How many things can you think of that we use in everyday life now that were not widely used in 1900? For example, how would your life be affected without:

electric light and power, central heating, computers, TVs, videos, music centres, batteries, planes, cars, motorways, cinemas, fast food, washing machines, dishwashers, microwaves?

In the 1990s it is easier to communicate all over the world.

1.1 THE FIRST WORLD WAR 1914–18

The great powers of Europe in 1914

In 1914 the great powers of Europe were Britain, France, Russia, Austria-Hungary, Germany and Italy. All the great powers were **rivals**. Each one wanted to be rich and powerful and have a big empire. Each one was afraid of the others. So each one wanted a big army and a big navy.

The alliances

Apart from building bigger armies and navies, the great powers made alliances. They agreed to help each other if they were attacked. The alliances were:

- The Triple Alliance: Austria-Hungary, Germany and Italy.
- The Triple Entente: Britain, France and Russia.

Source A

The spark for war?

It was summer 1914. All of Europe was tense. It only needed a small spark to set the great powers alight. The spark came on 28 June 1914. Franz Ferdinand was the son of the Austrian emperor. He was visiting Sarajevo in Serbia. He was shot by a Serb. The Austrians were furious. They invaded Serbia. But Russia was friendly with Serbia and went to help. Germany was friendly with Austria-Hungary, so gave it support. Then France joined in to help Russia.

The first move

Germany did not want to be caught between France and Russia. So Germany invaded France. The Germans wanted to defeat France quickly and then turn and fight Russia. To get to France the German army had to march through Belgium. Belgium was a friend of Britain's, so this brought Britain into the war. The only great power not to join in straightaway was Italy. Eventually Italy came in to help Britain, France and Russia because it wanted some of Austria-Hungary's territory.

Empires

The great powers had empires, so other countries were dragged into the war. On Britain's side many countries in the British Empire joined in, including Canada, Australia, New Zealand, India and South Africa.

An Italian cartoon. It shows the **Kaiser** of Germany greedy for an empire.

Where did they fight?

The Western Front
Germany's war to the west. Here Germany fought Britain, France, their colonies and (after 1917) the USA.

The trenches were on the Western Front.

Battle of Jutland
The only big battle at sea. Neither side a clear winner.

The Eastern Front
Germany's war to the East. Here Germany fought the Russians. There was no fixed line of battle here, the front line shifted back and forth over many miles. The Russians fought while they were also having a revolution which replaced their king with a communist government.

Submarines
The Germans used submarines to sink ships bringing supplies to Britain and her allies. When they sunk the *Lusitania*, a US passenger ship that was also carrying war supplies, the USA decided to join the war against Germany.

The Middle East
The war in the Middle East revolved around which side controlled the Suez Canal, which joined the Mediterranean to the Red Sea.

Italy
In 1914 Italy had been on Germany's side. In 1915 the Italians changed sides. So Germany had to fight Italy, too.

The Colonies
There was also fighting in the German colonies in Africa. The 3 colonies marked here were captured by the allies.

Who had what in 1914

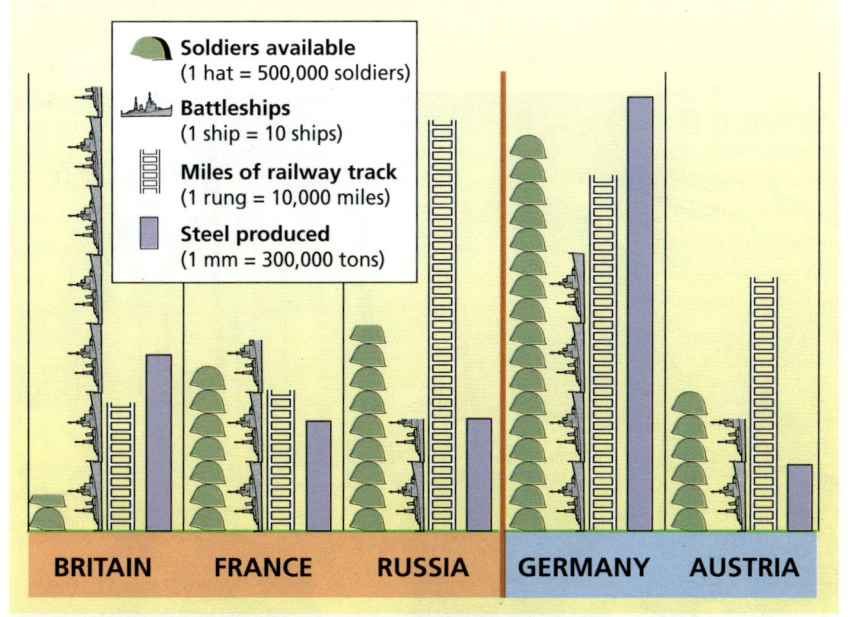

Key:
- Soldiers available (1 hat = 500,000 soldiers)
- Battleships (1 ship = 10 ships)
- Miles of railway track (1 rung = 10,000 miles)
- Steel produced (1 mm = 300,000 tons)

BRITAIN   FRANCE   RUSSIA   GERMANY   AUSTRIA

Questions

1 a Who were the six great powers of Europe in 1914?
b Why did each power want a bigger army and navy?

2 a What happened on the 28 June 1914?
b Why was it so important?

3 Why did Britain join the war?

1.2 THE FIRST WORLD WAR: THE TRENCHES

Over by Christmas?
Both sides expected the war to be over by Christmas. But it lasted for over four years. Why did it last so long?

Trenches
Trenches were ditches deep enough to protect the soldiers from being shot. The soldiers were not meant to stay in the trenches. However, it was soon clear that once they were in the trenches each side could pin the other side down with machine-gun fire. So the trenches became permanent. Some of the German trenches were lined with concrete and had electricity.

The Western Front
Soon trenches spread right across western Europe. Most fighting was done from the front line trenches in an area known as the Western Front. Behind them were support trenches and reserve trenches. Soldiers made their way to the front by trenches so they would not get shot.

No Man's Land
No Man's Land was the land between enemy trenches. Sometimes this was as little as 20 metres wide. Sometimes it was more than a kilometre wide. No Man's Land was fought over again and again.

Source A
A soldier remembers what it was like in the trenches.

All along the trench you'd have three men in a bay. One was on guard, one was cleaning up the trench and one was having a sleep. You changed round each hour. If the guard saw something, you all jumped up and started firing. That was at night. It was the same in the day, except you got the periscope out now and then, so you could see. We didn't bother much because Jerry [the Germans] didn't come across in daylight.

Source B
A painting by John Nash of a trench on the Western Front in 1918.

The fighting

When one side wanted to attack, they fired their big **artillery** guns at the enemy trenches. They hoped to break up the trenches and kill many enemy soldiers. After a few days of this, the attacking side sent its soldiers 'over the top' out of the trenches. They ran across No Man's Land to attack and try to take the enemy trenches. The problem was machine guns. The enemy laid low during the artillery raid. As soon as it was over, they set up their machine guns. Then they mowed down many of the soldiers running towards them.

New weapons

Gas: Poisonous gases attacked the eyes, lungs and nerves of people who breathed them in. Gas was first pumped into trenches in 1915. But if the wind changed, it could blow back on the soldiers. The invention of gas masks helped to protect soldiers and animals.

Tanks: Tanks were huge armed metal boxes on caterpillar tracks. They could cross rough ground and barbed wire. Machine guns did not bother them. However, they did get stuck in mud and they were a death trap if a shell or grenade hit them.

Planes: Planes were first used to find out where enemy soldiers were. Soon machine guns were put on planes so they could fight each other. Then in 1917 the Germans designed a plane that could carry bombs. The planes were dangerous to fly and the pilots had no parachutes.

Source C

Canadian soldiers at the third Battle of Ypres in 1917.

Source D

From a poem written by Siegfried Sassoon who fought in the trenches.

Sometimes he tripped and lurched
  against the walls.
With hands that pawed the sodden bags of chalk
He couldn't see the man who walked in front;
He only heard the drum and rattle of feet
Stepping along barred trench boards,
  often splashing
Wretchedly where the sludge was ankle deep.

Questions

1 What was a trench?

2 Why did the trenches become permanent?

3 Read **Source D**.
  a What were the trenches lined with according to this source?
  b Why was this?

4 a Why were tanks an important breakthrough?
  b Why would they have been useless in the conditions in **Source D**?

The Liverpool Scottish Battalion

Men joined the Liverpool Scottish Battalion to defend Britain if it was invaded. However, so many soldiers were needed at the front that the Battalion was soon sent to France to fight.

Robert Scott Macfie wrote letters home. Parts of some of his letters are shown below.

Numbers of soldiers killed, wounded or missing in three major offensives

Verdun (1916)	French:	550,000
	German:	434,000
Somme (1916)	French:	200,000
	German:	500,000
	British:	420,000
Third Battle of Ypres (1917)	British Empire:	310,000
	German:	300,000

Source E

Robert Scott Macfie.

The beginning
We have been told we go abroad on Friday 30 October. We are nowhere near ready: we have damaged rifles, many men are short of clothing and equipment. Lots of us are **recruits** and the rest are imperfectly trained. I never saw so incompetent a set of officers.

They got to France after a long boat and train journey.

Trenches
We have had our first practice digging trenches. They must be most uncomfortable in hot weather. I expect the scientific Germans will put in hot water radiators before the cold weather comes.

Moving up
We joined the remains of several regiments which have almost been wiped out. The farm where we are staying is a sea of mud.

Christmas 1914
It is Christmas Eve and we are all very homesick. The men are in an empty barn, cold and draughty. We are waiting to march off to even less comfortable lodgings, 'dugouts' – holes in the ground badly roofed and full of straw.

We went into the trenches cold and wet for there was heavy rain and snow as we marched. We wear whatever we can get, not smart uniforms, and have buckets and enamel cups and mugs tied to our belts with string. We do not march, we slouch along. Many men fall behind because they are lame.

Source F

The Liverpool Scottish, in action at Hooge.

The attack at Hooge, 16 June 1915
Macfie was in charge of the camp waiting for the soldiers to return.

We got tea and pea soup going on the cookers. One hundred and thirty of my company had left: I was ready to feed them when they got back.

At last we heard the sound of pipes. A handful of men came through the gate. Their uniforms were tattered, their faces blackened and unshaven, their clothes stained red with blood and yellow with the fumes of gas. I shouted for Y Company – only one man came forward. Gradually others tottered in. By 5.30 am there were 25 of my men in camp. I have found out that 11 were killed, 68 are in hospital and 25 are missing. I fear most are dead.

The Battle of the Somme, 1916
Our attack, in the early hours of 9 August, was against a village which had been attacked before without success. We did not take it either. Of my company 177 went up – 20 were killed, 42 wounded and about 8 missing, probably dead. The lack of preparation, the vague orders, the ignorance of what we were supposed to do, even of the geography of the place, the absurd haste, the horrid mistakes – it was a scandal. In any well-run organisation one of the commanders would have been shot.

1.3 COWARDS AND TRAITORS?

Fighting for King and Country

In 1914 there were about 164,000 men in the British army. By 1916 there were over two million men. Was everyone keen to fight?

There was a lot of pressure on young men to fight for their country. Ordinary people stopped young men in the street and asked them why they were not in uniform. Some people handed out white feathers, which were a sign of being a coward. Even so some men felt it was wrong to fight.

Conscription

From the beginning of the war, huge numbers of men were killed or wounded. More and more soldiers were needed. By 1916 it was obvious that all young men were going to have to fight.

The government brought in conscription. This meant that all single men between the ages of 18 and 41 had to join one of the forces, unless they were doing important war work. The government also said that men who had a **conscientious** objection to fighting did not have to join up either. This could be because of religion or because they believed in peace. Some men refused to fight because of their religious beliefs and some because they did not believe in killing other human beings.

Tribunals

Tribunals were made up of important local people. Conscientious objectors had to explain to them why they did not want to fight. The Tribunal had to decide whether they were genuine or cowards.

Conchies

'Conchie' was the short name given to a conscientious objector. There were about 16,000 conchies. Many refused to fight but went to war as ambulance drivers or stretcher carriers.

About 1500 said they would have nothing to do with the war at all. Some of those were sent to prison. A few were shot.

Source A

TO THE YOUNG WOMEN OF LONDON

Is your "Best Boy" wearing Khaki? If not don't YOU THINK he should be?

If he does not think that you and your country are worth fighting for—do you think he is WORTHY of you?

Don't pity the girl who is alone—her young man is probably a soldier—fighting for her and her country—and for YOU.

If your young man neglects his duty to his King and Country, the time may come when he will NEGLECT YOU.

Think it over—then ask him to

JOIN THE ARMY TO-DAY

Pressure to join up

Government posters encouraged men to fight to protect their country and their families. There were some posters showing how wicked and evil the enemy was, and declaring that everyone must fight against evil.

A poster pressurising women to get their boyfriends to join up.

ONE 'CONCHIE'S' WAR

Howard Marten lived in London. He was a **Quaker**. Quakers did not believe in fighting.

He was forced to join the Non-Combatant Corps and drive ambulances to help the war in that way. He was put in prison for refusing to obey orders. Then he was shipped to France.

Marten and four others were court-martialled for disobedience. Marten wondered what would happen to him. He was led to the parade ground to hear the verdict.

There were lots of men lined up. We were taken to one side of the parade ground, then led out, one by one into the middle of the square. I was the first of them. An officer in charge read out the various crimes. Then the sentence of the court was that we were to suffer death by being shot. There was a pause. I thought 'Well, that's that'. Then he said, 'Confirmed by the Commander in Chief'. Then after a long pause: 'But commuted to penal servitude [prison] in England for ten years.'

And that was that. What was good was that we were back in England and out of the hands of the army.

Marten was released from prison to work in a stone quarry near Aberdeen.

Source B

Howard Marten, photographed with his mother and Cornie Barret, one of the other 'conchies' sentenced to death with him.

Questions

1. a What was a conscientious objector?
   b What is conscription?

2. Read **One 'conchie's' war**.
   a Why was Marten a conscientious objector?
   b Do you think conscientious objectors were just cowards? Explain the reasons for your view.

3. Read **Source A**.
   How does the poster put pressure on girls to ask their boyfriends to join up?

What the war was really like

Soldiers knew that the war was really bad. They had lived and fought in the trenches. They knew the disease, the mud and the death. It was not glorious to go and fight on the Western Front. But when they came home on leave they found that everyone back home still thought that it was glamorous and exciting. Most soldiers did not want to tell their families and friends how bad it was. So they pretended that everything was fine.

What to do about the war

After they had been on leave, most soldiers went back to fight on the Western Front. They just got on with it. But some men found the senseless slaughter too much. Some ran away. These were called deserters. Some refused to obey orders. These were called mutineers. Deserters and mutineers were shot. It was meant to be a lesson to all other soldiers.

This painting of the Western Front was by C.W.R. Nevison. It was not finished until 1921. He would probably not have been allowed to show it in war time.

SIEGFRIED SASSOON

The English poet Siegfried Sassoon joined up as soon as the war started. He became a very good officer. He was awarded the Military Cross for bravery.

Poetry and criticism of the war

Sassoon wrote poetry about the horrors of war. He also criticised the generals. He said that they threw away men's lives by not thinking out their attacks. In 1917, he was so angry that he threw away his Military Cross. He also wrote to *The Times* newspaper. His letter caused trouble. He said:

I believe the war is being deliberately prolonged by those who have the power to end it.

Shell shock and survival

Sassoon was a brave soldier. He had won a medal. It was difficult for the army. They tried to persuade him to think again. They also said that he was shell-shocked and put him in an army hospital. In fact Sassoon began to feel that he could not stop the war. He felt he was letting his soldiers down. He went back to the front and carried on fighting. He survived the war and became a famous poet.

Source C

Source D

An Australian recruiting poster. Troops from all over the colonies fought in the war. Some of them, like the Canadians, accepted the British army could court-martial their men. Others, like the Australians, did not.

Australia has promised Britain 50,000 MORE MEN WILL YOU HELP US KEEP THAT PROMISE

Who was shot?

Between 1914 and 1916, 346 men were shot for military crimes. Most of these were ordinary soldiers. Many of them had been fighting for months. They had seen terrible suffering. They had seen friends killed and wounded. Many of them could not take any more.

Source E

Captain Slack was an officer in the East Yorkshire Regiment. He had to organise at least one firing squad.

There was one poor little man who came to me. He ran away. He was caught and ran away again. He was court-martialled for desertion and sentenced to be shot. My Sergeant-Major and I had to pick ten men to shoot him and one of my officers had to be in charge with a revolver.

The man was shot. I wrote to his mother 'killed in action'. I think that's what they were all told. It was a horrible thing to have to do, but it had to be done.

Questions

1. What was a deserter?
2. What was a mutineer?
3. Read **Source E**.
   a. If you were in a firing squad, how would you have felt about shooting a deserter?
   b. Why do you think the mother was told that her son had been killed in action?

1.4 THE SUFFRAGETTES GO TO WAR

Suffrage

Suffrage means the right to vote. By 1900 most men in Britain had the right to vote, but no women had that right. Women who worked to get the right to vote were called suffragists or suffragettes.

The National Union of Women's Suffrage Societies – Suffragists

This was set up in the 1860s. The women gave talks and wrote letters to important people. They wanted to persuade people that women should have the vote.

The Women's Social and Political Union – Suffragettes

This was set up in 1903 by the Pankhurst family. They did not feel that letters and talks were getting anywhere.

Their motto was 'Deeds not Words'. They had marches and ran a newspaper. Lots of women, rich and poor, joined the WSPU. But still Parliament did not give women the vote.

The suffragettes did more and more outrageous things. They smashed windows, chained themselves to railings and got arrested. In jail they went on hunger strike. All of this brought them a lot of publicity.

Support

More and more people began to think that women should have the vote. But by the time of the First World War, some suffragettes had become so violent that they were unpopular.

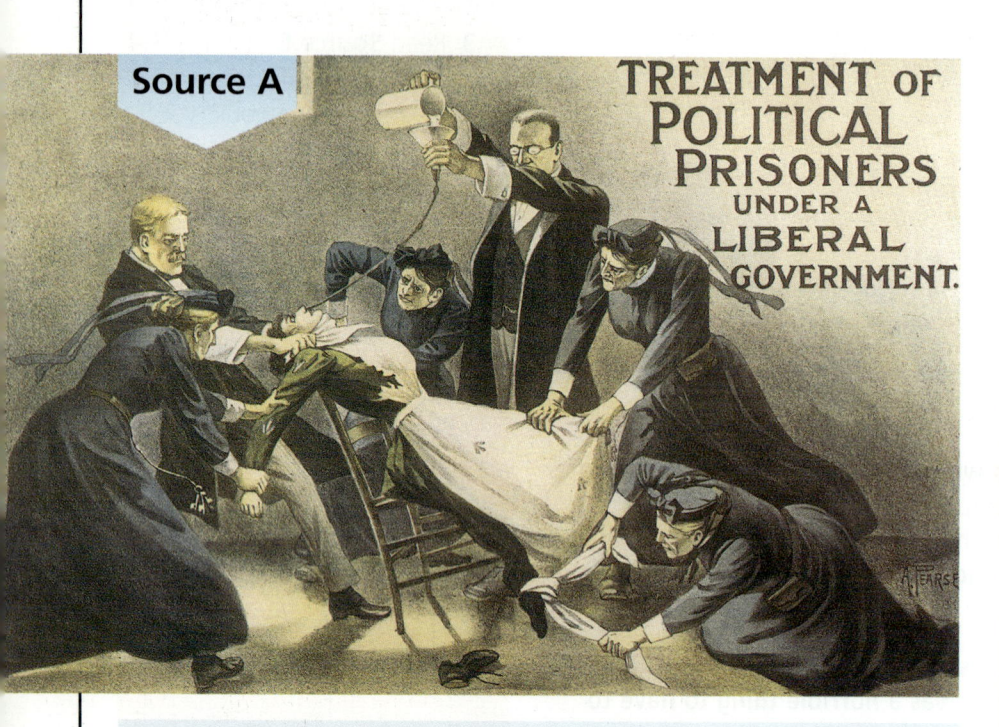

Source A

Some suffragettes went on hunger strike in prison. They were force-fed. This action horrified many people.

Questions

1. What is suffrage?
2. a When was the WSPU set up?
   b What was the WSPU's motto?
   c What do you think this motto means?
3. Make a WSPU poster using their colours (purple, green and white). It should tell people how they can work to get the vote.

Source B

These suffragettes are demonstrating outside Buckingham Palace in 1914.

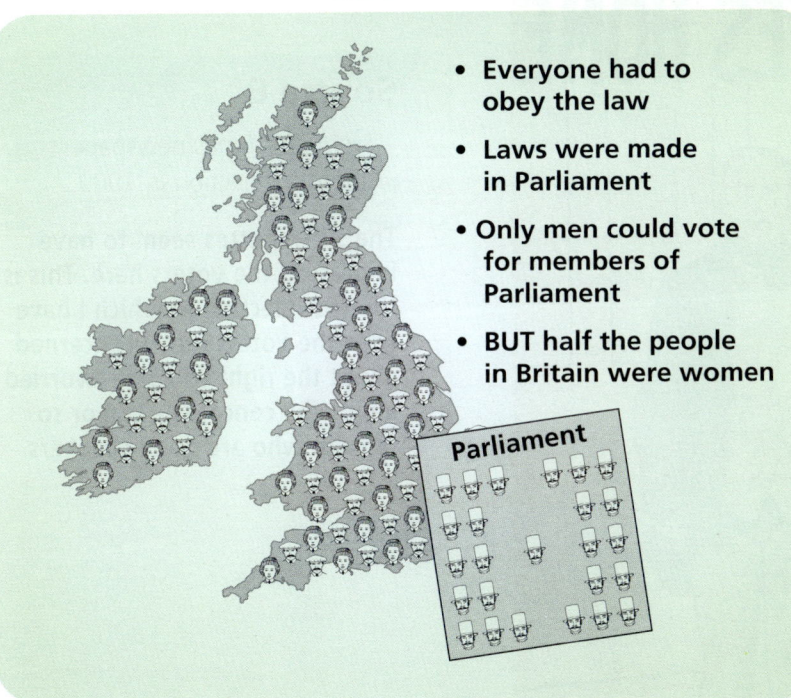

- Everyone had to obey the law
- Laws were made in Parliament
- Only men could vote for members of Parliament
- BUT half the people in Britain were women

Parliament

THE PANKHURSTS

Emmeline Pankhurst and her daughters, Christabel, Sylvia and Adela, set up the WSPU in 1903. Sylvia and Adela wanted to push for all women to get the vote. Christabel argued that it was better to get the vote for well-off respectable women first.

EMILY DAVISON

Emily Davison was a famous suffragette. She was a militant. She smashed windows and set fire to pillar boxes. She was arrested several times. She went on hunger strike and was force-fed.

In 1913 she went to the Derby, a famous horse race. She ran on to the racetrack to stop the king's horse. She was trampled and died four days later. The suffragettes gave her a huge funeral and said she had died for the cause of women's votes.

Against votes for women

Some men and women were against votes for women. This is what one wrote:

Suffragettes ignore man's superior strength. They ignore man's superior mind. They ignore man's superior money earning.

In support of votes for women

Many women and men supported votes for women. This is what one wrote:

Because it is the foundation of all political liberty that those who obey the Law should be able to have a voice in choosing who makes the Law.

Source D

A SUFFRAGETTE'S HOME

AFTER A HARD DAY'S WORK!

Published by the Campaign Committee, National League for Opposing Woman Suffrage, Caxton House, Westminster. JOIN!

Source C

A rhyme made up for a poster against women getting the vote.

This is The House that Man built,

The House that our statesmen for years have controlled,

Ruling the world with mind fearless and bold.

Can Woman expect to rule such a House?

She that's afraid of a poor little mouse:

No, No Suffragette your place is not yet

Inside The House that man built.

Source E

From *The Times* newspaper about an election in 1909.

The suffragettes seem to have impressed the voters here. This is the first election in which I have seen the voters really concerned about the right to vote – worried about the concerns of 20 or so women who are good speakers.

A poster from the time against women getting the vote. Women as well as men joined societies against the suffragettes.

Source F

SUFFRAGETTES BURN ST. CATHERINE'S CHURCH, HATCHAM!!

DAILY BLAH

- Burning a church! I used to support them, not any more!
- I agree. They've gone too far.
- I know they need publicity, but people could have been hurt!
- No, they made sure the church was empty first.
- I used to belong to the WSPU, but I resigned. I want the vote, but I won't be violent.
- I hear there are more moderate movements. Join one of them.
- A woman should stay at home and mind her own business. Politics is men's work.
- They're all the same. They should be banned.

Opinion on suffragettes in 1913.

Questions

1 Read page 114.
  a What were the three arguments given against votes for women?
  b Write down the argument given for votes for women.

2 Read **Source C**.
  a What is The House that man built?
  b What argument is given against women being allowed into The House?
  c Is there any hope in the poem that women may some day get in?

Women needed

When the First World War started many men joined up. As the war went on, more and more men were needed to fight. This meant that women were needed to do men's jobs.

The jobs

Women took on every sort of job. They drove buses, mined coal, farmed, nursed, made guns, bombs and tanks, trained horses for the army, drove ambulances, swept chimneys and made steel. It was found that women were about two-thirds as strong as men. So if a job in a steel works took two men, then three women could do the job. Since women were always paid less money, even for the same amount of work, no one minded.

The right to serve

Mrs Emmeline Pankhurst was a good organiser. She had organised the suffragettes. So the government asked her to organise women to take up war work. Mrs Pankhurst said yes for two reasons:

- She believed that the Germans had to be defeated.
- She believed that if women did war work well, they would show the government that they were as good as men.

After the war

The government said women could have the vote. Having seen the work they had done in the war it was hard to argue that they were too silly and ignorant to vote. Also the government wanted women to give back their jobs to men. They did not want a fuss.

Laws for women's rights

1870 Married women could keep their earnings.

1882 Married women could own property (everything from clothes to houses).

1888 Women could vote in local elections.

1907 Women could become local councillors.

1918 Vote given to women over the age of thirty who were householders or wives of householders.

1928 Vote given to all women over the age of twenty-one.

A Right to Serve march, 17 July 1915.

Source G

Source H

THE SUFFRAGETTES IN WAR

It was August 1914. Mairi Chisholm was eighteen years old. She rode from Scotland to London on her motorbike to look for war work.

At first she delivered messages. Then she went to the Western Front as a nurse but she was miles behind the lines. She met another nurse called Elsie Knocker. They set up a first-aid post just behind the front line. They could now help wounded soldiers straight away.

We helped soldiers, but we also had to try to rescue the pilots who were brought down in No Man's Land. That was what we got the Military Medal for, you see. We went on foot. There weren't always stretchers, we had to hope to get them out with their arms around our necks. I strained a valve in my heart lugging men around on my back. We had an ambulance of our own and I'd drive them back in that. You had to do it in stops and spurts, being shot at.

As well as dealing with the wounded we got men in from the trenches with boils, sore feet, all sorts of things. We slept in our clothes.

Mairi Chisholm and Elsie Knocker in Belgium.

CAROLINE RENNLES

Caroline Rennles worked in London, making bombs. The TNT in the bombs had a strange effect:

It turned the hair that stuck out from our caps ginger, and our skin yellow. They used to call us 'canaries'. Some people were nice to us, but others used to treat us like scum. We didn't realise it was dangerous. Tram conductors used to say, 'You'll be dead in two years.' So we said, 'We don't mind dying for our country.' We were young and patriotic.

Questions

1 What kind of war work did women do?

2 Why did Emmeline Pankhurst agree to organise war work?

3 Why did the government give women the vote in 1918? Give two reasons.

1.5 THE TREATY OF VERSAILLES

What happens after a war?
After a war countries meet to decide what will happen to the losers. Often it is only the winners who meet to decide what will happen to the losers. This is what happened after the First World War.

The Treaty of Versailles
In 1919, representatives from 32 countries travelled to Versailles in France to decide what would happen to the defeated countries: Germany, Austria-Hungary, Turkey and Bulgaria. These countries had no say in what happened to them. Russia was left out of making the decisions because it had made peace with Germany in 1917. This had made the others angry.

The Big Three
There were many countries represented at Versailles. But the decisions were taken by the most powerful countries: Britain, the United States and France.

What did the Big Three want?
- France wanted revenge and **compensation** for those who were killed and the damage. (Much of the war was fought in France.)
- The United States wanted a fair peace that would stop future wars in Europe.
- Britain wanted the Germans punished, but did not want the punishment to be too harsh in case the Germans were so angry they started another war.

Wilson
Wanted a lasting peace and no more war.

Clemenceau
Wanted revenge on Germany.

Lloyd George
Wanted Germany punished but not too harshly.

Questions
1. Which were the four defeated countries?
2. Which other country was not allowed to come to Versailles? Why?
3. Who were the Big Three?
4. Look at the box headed **The Treaty of Versailles**.
   a. Which of the Big Three countries would be most happy with the treaty?
   b. What was the reason behind decision 4?
   c. What was the reason behind decision 5?
   d. What was the reason behind decision 6?
   e. Which decision might be very hard for the Germans to stick to after the war? Give your reasons.

Source A
Harold Nicholson was a British representative at Versailles. He said:

The historian will come to the conclusion that we were very stupid men.

What happened?

Talks went on at Versailles for six months. Then the Treaty of Versailles was presented to the Germans to sign.

What the Germans thought

The German leader was appalled. He resigned.

What the Germans were told

The Germans were told that if they did not sign the treaty, their country would be invaded.

Europe after the Treaty of Versailles.

Legend:
- Territory lost by Germany to other countries
- Territory lost by Germany to the League of Nations
- Area formerly Austria-Hungary
- Area formerly owned by Russia
- Demilitarized zone

The Treaty of Versailles

1. The war was Germany's fault.

2. Germany had to pay for the war damage.

3. Germany lost its colonies and part of its land.

4. The Germans were allowed a small army (100,000 men), no airforce, a small navy, no tanks or submarines.

5. Germany could not have an army or forts within 50 kilometres of France.

6. Territory that Russia had given to Germany was formed into new countries.

Other decisions

- Austria-Hungary was split in two.

- Yugoslavia and Czechoslovakia were set up.

- Turkey lost land in Europe.

2.1 THE RISE OF THE DICTATORS

After the First World War there were a lot of changes in Germany, Russia and Italy. In different ways they all came to be ruled by **dictators**.

Russia before 1917

Until 1917, Russia was ruled by Tsar Nicholas II. He was helped by his nobles. But 95 per cent of Russian people had no say in making the laws they had to obey or in running the country. Five per cent of the people (mostly nobles) were rich. But everyone else worked hard and most were very poor.

Unrest before 1917

Gradually people began to complain about how the Tsar ran the country and how poor most people were. In 1905 there was a revolution. The Tsar was very worried. He agreed to have an elected parliament called the Duma. In this parliament the Russian people could help make laws. But soon the revolution fizzled out. Then the Tsar ignored the parliament.

War

Russia went to war in 1914. The war went on and on. Thousands and thousands of Russian soldiers died. The Tsar went to the front to encourage and lead his soldiers. Back home he left his German wife and her holy man, Rasputin, in charge. The nobles did not like Rasputin and murdered him.

The end of the Tsar

Things went from bad to worse. The Russian soldiers wanted to go home. The ordinary people were hungry. There was a revolution in March 1917. The Tsar was forced to **abdicate**. The new government did not last long. It was overthrown by a political party called the Bolsheviks led by Lenin. After killing the Tsar and his family and fighting against other groups who wanted to rule Russia, the Bolsheviks won.

RASPUTIN

Rasputin came from a poor Russian family in the country. He was very **charismatic**. People would follow him and believe what he said. He became known as a holy man and a healer. The Tsar's only son, Alexei, had a rare blood disease. It was called haemophilia. He could die of the simplest cut. Rasputin seemed to help him. Then he moved on to help run the country. That is when the Russian nobles poisoned him and threw him in the river.

A Bolshevik poster. It shows the Tsar, the Church and the nobles riding on the shoulders of ordinary Russian people.

Source A

The Soviet Union

Lenin changed the name of Russia to the Soviet Union. He renamed his party the Communist Party. He stayed in power until 1924, when he died.

Trotsky and Stalin

After Lenin's death there was a power struggle between two of his followers. One was Trotsky, the other was Stalin. Stalin won. He exiled Trotsky and later had him murdered. The Soviet Union became a great power and Stalin ruled with an iron hand. The Communist Party was the only political party allowed. Stalin was ruthless with those who were against him. As many as 20 million people may have died for opposing him.

Italy

After the First World War, Italy was poor. There were very few jobs. Many people did not like what was happening in the Soviet Union. They were afraid that there might be a communist revolution in Italy. Mussolini promised this would not happen.

Fascism – follow the leaders

Mussolini said that ordinary people should follow their leaders. They should do as they were told so that Italy could become a strong, rich country. The sort of rights they had to give up were having trade unions and free speech in the newspapers.

The march on Rome

In 1922 thousands of Mussolini's supporters marched on Rome. They demanded that Mussolini be made prime minister. The king agreed.

Mussolini and power

Mussolini took more and more power. He banned any other political parties. He put opponents in prison. He did make some things run better in Italy, such as farming and industry. But he had grand ideas about making a new Roman Empire and dragged Italy into the Second World War. Italy was defeated.

Source B

Mussolini wanted to be Italy's new Roman emperor.

Questions

1. What was the name of the Russian Tsar?
2. Who led the Bolshevik Party?
3. Why do you think so many people opposed Stalin?
4. What rights did Mussolini expect ordinary Italian people to give up?

Germany lost the war

Germany was defeated in the First World War. The German Emperor was Kaiser Wilhelm. He abdicated and went to live abroad. Now Germany had to recover from the war.

The Weimar Republic

The new German government was called the Weimar Republic. It was faced with many problems.

- The German people blamed the new government for signing the hated Treaty of Versailles.
- Not only did the Germans hate losing the war, they also hated paying huge sums of money for war damage to the countries that had won the war. This money was called reparations.
- There was lots of unrest. Several times groups tried to overthrow the government. This happened in 1919. The government only just defeated a communist group called the Sparticists. Then in 1920 a Dr Kapp took control in Berlin for a short while. In 1923 a young man called Adolf Hitler tried to take over the government. He failed and went to prison.

Source C

A Nazi poster showing Hitler saving Germany.

Germany stops paying reparations, 1923

By 1923 Germany could not afford to pay the huge sums of money to France and other countries. It just stopped paying. France was furious. French soldiers marched into Germany. They took over the Ruhr. This was an area where there were many coal mines and steel works. France said that if Germany did not pay reparations, they would take the coal and steel and sell it for themselves.

Inflation

The German economy collapsed. There was massive **inflation** and it took more and more money to buy things. In the end people had to take a wheelbarrow to work to collect their week's wages. Then the week's wages bought no more than a loaf of bread. This made people hate the government more.

Gustav Stresemann

Stresemann was a remarkable man. He became Chancellor (Prime Minister) in 1923. He brought in a new currency which helped end inflation. Then he worked to gain the confidence of other countries. People trusted him and he achieved three important things:

- The French withdrew from the Ruhr.
- Germany joined the League of Nations.
- The USA lent Germany money to build up industries and factories.

The Crash, 1929

Germany started doing well, but disasters occurred in 1929. Gustav Stresemann died. Then the stock market crashed in the USA. The USA had no money. It demanded that Germany repay the loans for industries and factories. German factory owners and business men went bankrupt. And the one man, Stresemann, who might have persuaded the USA to hold back, was dead.

Unemployment in Germany

German unemployment went from under a million to over six million. People were desperate. They turned to Adolf Hitler and the Nazi Party. Hitler said:

- He would create jobs.
- He would tear up the Treaty of Versailles.
- He would get back Germany's lost land.

Here, at last, was someone who would make Germany rich and strong again.

Hitler as Chancellor

The Nazi Party won the most seats in the Reichstag (German Parliament) in 1932. Then in 1933, Hitler was made Chancellor.

What Hitler and the Nazi Party believed:

- The Treaty of Versailles should be torn up.
- Germany should have a strong government.
- Germany should seize more land in Eastern Europe.
- The Germans were the master race.
- Jews should not be allowed to be Germans.

Questions

1 After the war what was the new government in Germany called?

2 What did the German people blame the new government for?

3 Do you think **Source C** is a good poster? Explain why.

4 What were the things that Adolf Hitler said he would do for Germany?

5 Why would this win him votes?

What Hitler did to keep control

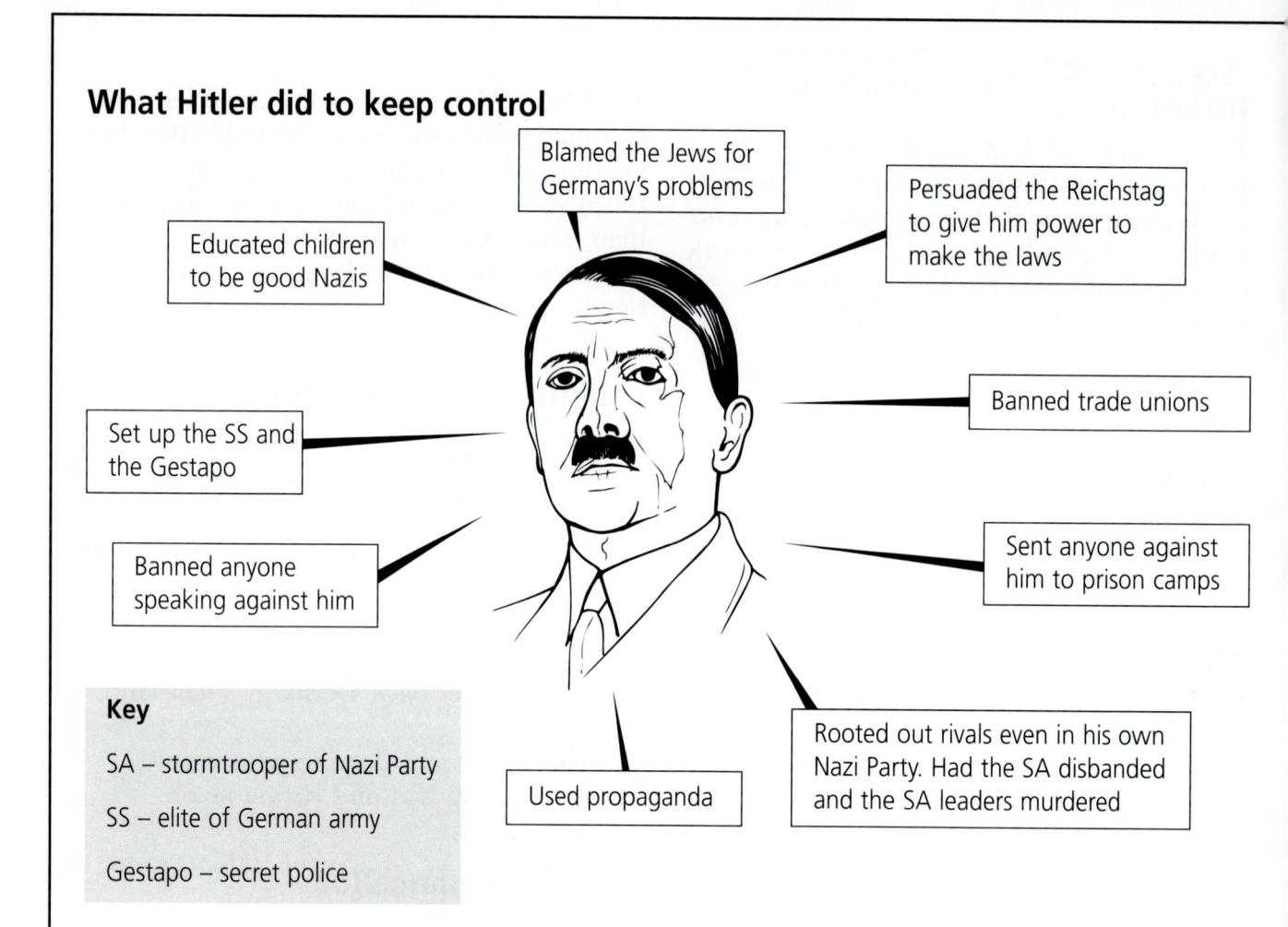

- Blamed the Jews for Germany's problems
- Persuaded the Reichstag to give him power to make the laws
- Educated children to be good Nazis
- Banned trade unions
- Set up the SS and the Gestapo
- Banned anyone speaking against him
- Sent anyone against him to prison camps
- Used propaganda
- Rooted out rivals even in his own Nazi Party. Had the SA disbanded and the SA leaders murdered

Key

SA – stormtrooper of Nazi Party

SS – elite of German army

Gestapo – secret police

A timetable from a girls' school in Nazi Germany.

Source D

Periods	Monday	Tuesday	Wednesday	Thursday	Friday	Saturday
8:00 – 8:45	German	German	German	German	German	German
8:50 – 9:35	Geography	History	Singing	Geography	History	Singing
9:40 – 10:25	Race study	Race study	Race study	Ideology	Ideology	Ideology
10:25 – 11:00	Recess, with sports and special announcements					
11:00 – 12:05	Domestic science with maths	Domestic science with maths	Domestic science with maths	Domestic science with maths	Domestic science with maths	Domestic science with maths
12:10 – 12:55	Eugenics	Health Biology	Eugenics	Health Biology	Eugenics	Health Biology

Source E

A fund-raising poster for the Hitler Youth.

Source F

From a newspaper article. It was written by David Lloyd George, who had been the British Prime Minister at the Treaty of Versailles. He met Hitler in 1936.

I have just returned from Germany. Whatever one thinks of Hitler's methods – and they are certainly not those of a parliamentary country – there can be no doubt that he has achieved a marvellous change in the spirit of the people, in their attitude towards each other and in their economic outlook. He is a born leader of men. He is also securing them against the constant fear of starvation, which is one of the worst memories of war and the first years of peace.

What Hitler did to keep power

Propaganda

Hitler used propaganda a lot. Propaganda is like advertising. It is designed to make people think in a certain way. Hitler made Joseph Goebbels head of a government department for propaganda. His job was to advertise Hitler and the Nazi Party over and over again. He did this in these ways.

- He ran poster campaigns.
- He ran newspapers and made other newspapers write good things about the Nazis.
- He had radio programmes made.
- He and Hitler and other Nazi leaders made speeches.
- He had films made.
- He had whispering campaigns started. (People will often believe rumours rather than news stories).

Children

Another way Hitler kept power was through education in schools. Children were taught how wonderful Hitler and the Nazi Party were. History books were rewritten to show that the Germans were the master race. They also showed that Jews were to blame for all Germany's problems. Outside school, children were expected to join Hitler Youth groups. Boys must grow up to be healthy soldiers. Girls must grow up to be good, healthy mothers.

Questions

1. **a** What did Hitler persuade the Reichstag to do?
   b What happened to anyone who was against Hitler?
   c What did Hitler set up to keep control?

2. Read **Source F**.
   What three things did Lloyd George say Hitler had achieved?

The League of Nations

Germany joined the League of Nations in 1924.

The League had been set up after the First World War. It was made up of important countries.

The League was supposed to stop war ever happening again. But that meant that the countries in the League might have to send soldiers to stop a war. None of them was keen to do that.

In 1931 Japan attacked China. The League did not stop it happening.

In 1933 Italy attacked Abyssinia. The League did not stop this happening either.

In the same year Hitler decided to take Germany out of the League of Nations.

Hitler goes back on the terms of the Treaty of Versailles

Leaving the League of Nations was just a start. Hitler was determined Germany would be strong again.

He began to build up the German airforce (Luftwaffe). He also built up the army.

Then in 1936 he sent German soldiers to take back the Rhineland.

He was not allowed to do any of these things under the terms of the Treaty of Versailles.

But no one stopped him. Britain and France did not want war. Some people also thought that Germany had been unfairly treated under the Treaty of Versailles, so what Hitler was doing was only fair.

Land Germany gained, 1933–9.

Reasons for the outbreak of war.

- Failure of appeasement
- Resentment of Versailles Treaty
- Hitler's aggression
- Weakness of League

Hitler and the road to war

Austria

In 1938 Hitler sent German soldiers into Austria. He said the two countries were now one country. Britain and France complained but did nothing.

Czechoslovakia – Sudetenland, 1938

Next Hitler looked towards Czechoslovakia.

Three million Germans lived in a part of Czechoslovakia called the Sudetenland. Hitler said he must have the Sudetenland as part of Germany.

Britain, France and Italy agreed that Germany could have the Sudetenland.

This decision was popular in Britain. It meant there would not be a war.

For his part Hitler said that he did not want any more terriitory in Europe.

The rest of Czechoslovakia

Six months later, Hitler sent German soldiers to seize the rest of Czechoslovakia.

Britain and France were shocked. Hitler was not to be trusted. They realised that Poland would be next.

Britain and France agreed to help Poland if Germany attacked.

War

On 1 September 1939, Hitler sent German soldiers into Poland. Two days later Britain and France declared war on Germany.

*Q*uestion

Why did Britain and France not go to war when Hitler invaded the Sudetenland?

2.2 THE SECOND WORLD WAR

On 1 September 1939 German dive bombers and tanks began attacking Poland. Britain and France declared war on 3 September and the Second World War began. But nothing more happened for six months. Then Germany overran Denmark, Norway, Holland and Belgium. In May 1940 Germany carried on into France.

Dunkirk and the fall of France

The lines of British and French soldiers protecting France were cut in two. One half was trapped in the north at Dunkirk. Thousands of small boats helped to ferry soldiers back to Britain. In all 338,000 British and French soldiers were rescued.

Vichy France

Germany took over northern France and left the French to rule southern France from the town of Vichy, although the Vichy government was really under German control.

The war in Europe and North Africa, 1939–42.

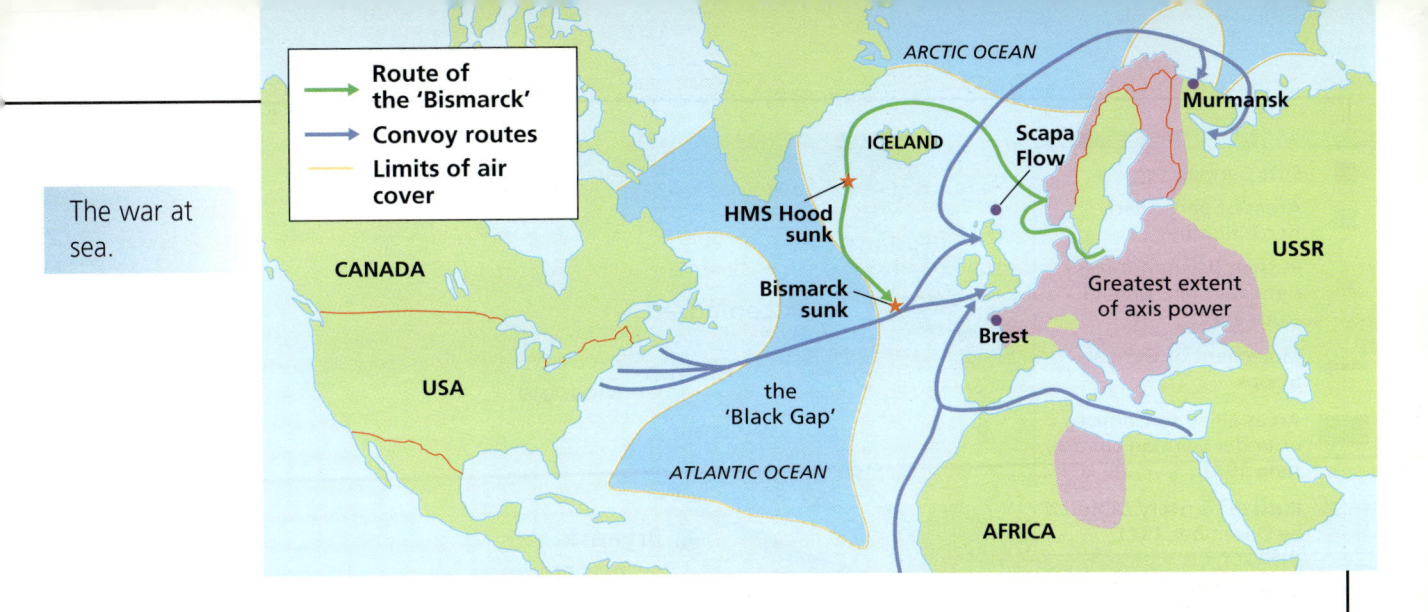

The war at sea.

The Axis powers
Germany and Italy were allies at the start of the war. They were called the Axis powers.

Britain alone
By 1940 Britain was the only country left fighting Germany. But Britain was not going to last long unless ships brought in from other countries the food, guns and everything else needed to fight a war.

U-boats and convoys
The German aim was to sink as many British ships as possible. Then Britain would have to surrender. British ships sailed in groups known as convoys with destroyers to protect them. The ships carried everything from petrol and aeroplanes to meat and sugar. The German submarines (U-boats) sailed from French ports. They attacked the convoys far out to sea. Sometimes they sank about one in every four British ships.

Sonar and code breaking
Two things helped to turn the war at sea in Britain's favour. The invention of **sonar** meant that submarines could be detected and the breaking of German secret codes meant that the British could read German messages.

Questions
1 Look at the map **The war in Europe and North Africa, 1939–42**.
   a Who were Germany's allies?
   b Which countries were conquered by Germany? Write in the dates as well.
2 Why was it so important that Britain developed radar and broke the German secret codes?

Legend:
- 🟥 First German targets
- 🟦 Areas of particularly fierce fighting
- ⭐ Russian partisan forces fight Germans behind front lines
- ➡ Movement of German troops
- 🟩 Areas allied to Germany or under German control, June 1941
- 🟧 Russian territory captured by December 1941

Operation Barbarossa.

The war with Russia

Hitler wanted to defeat Russia. He hated communism. He wanted more land for German people to live in. He also wanted the **oilfields** in Russia.

Operation Barbarossa

In 1941 Germany invaded Russia. At first all went well. By the end of 1941, German soldiers had reached Leningrad (now called St Petersburg). They had captured the factories and rich farmland of the Ukraine and they were near Moscow. Then winter came. It was so cold that the oil froze in the engines of vehicles. The German army could not advance further. It was not until June 1942 that they renewed their attempt to capture Moscow and the Russian oilfields.

Stalingrad (now called Volgograd)

The Germans wanted to take Stalingrad. They laid siege to the city for five months. The Russians were starving but they held out and the Germans had to surrender. After this the Russians steadily pushed the Germans back. By the end of 1944 all Russian land had been recaptured and the Russians were pushing on into Germany itself.

The expansion of Japan.

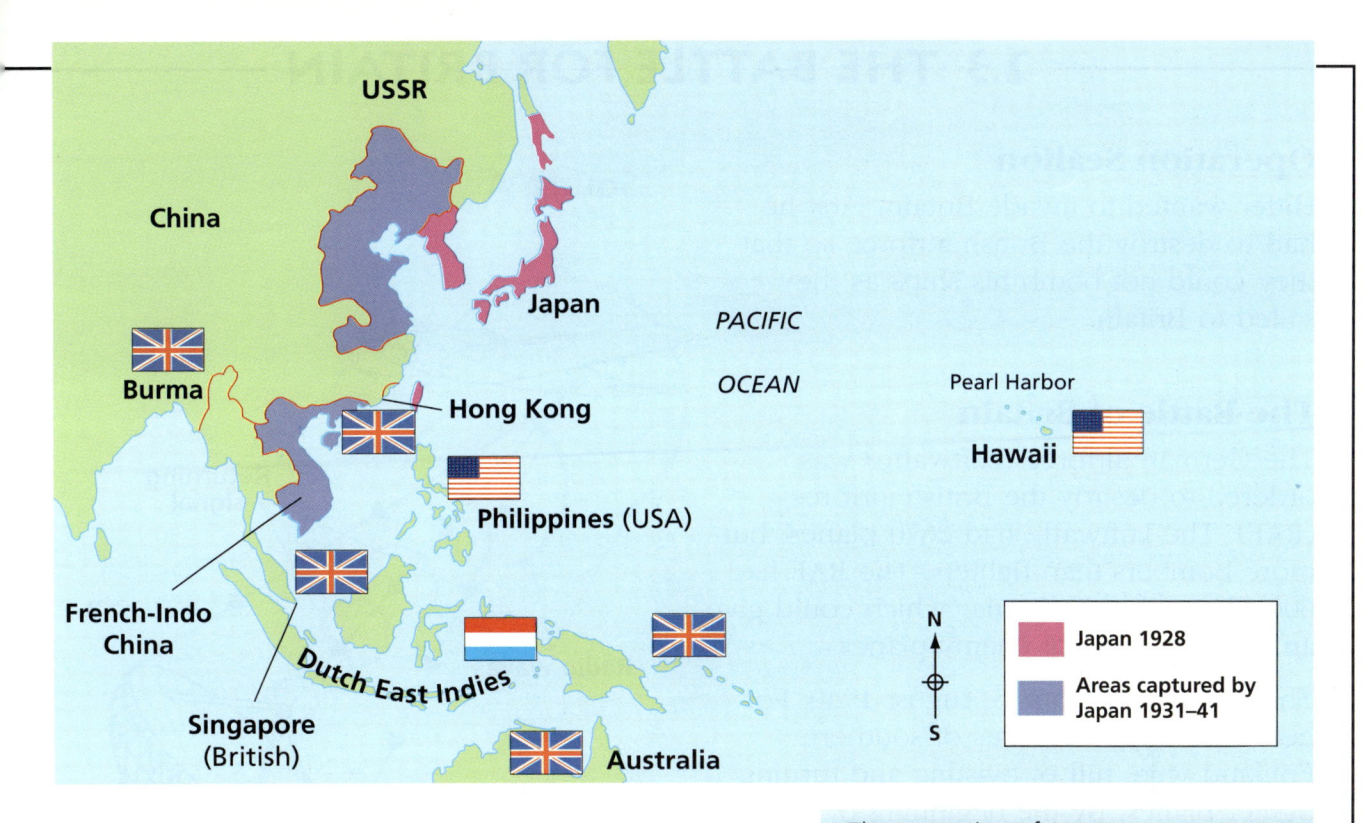

The war in the Far East

Japan wanted an empire. By 1941, Japan controlled a great deal of eastern China. But to build up a really big empire in the Far East meant fighting other countries. Britain, France, Holland and the USA all had interests in the Far East.

Britain, France, Holland and the USA

France and Holland had been overrun by Germany. Britain was alone fighting for survival. Neither of them could do anything to stop Japan. The USA was a different matter. Japan knew that the USA might use her large navy to stop Japan gaining land in the Far East.

Pearl Harbor

The Japanese decided to strike first. The USA kept a huge fleet at Pearl Harbor in the Hawaiian Islands. Secretly the Japanese sailed towards Hawaii. Then on Sunday, 7 December 1941, 400 Japanese planes took off from their aircraft carriers. They sank or badly damaged 18 ships. They killed about 3000 Americans. It was this attack that brought the USA into the war on Britain's side.

Questions

1 Read **Operation Barbarossa**.
   a Why did Hitler want to invade Russia in 1941?
   b Where had the German armies reached by the end of 1941?
   c What stopped the Germans going any further by the end of 1941?
   d How long was it before they advanced again?
   e Apart from the terrible winter, what other problems do you think an army would have fighting so far from home?

2 Read **The war in the Far East**.
   a Why did Japan bomb Pearl Harbor?
   b What was the result of the bombing of Pearl Harbor?

2.3 THE BATTLE FOR BRITAIN

Operation Sealion

Hitler wanted to invade Britain. First he had to destroy the British airforce so that they could not bomb his ships as they sailed to Britain.

The Battle of Britain

The German airforce (Luftwaffe) was ordered to destroy the British airforce (RAF). The Luftwaffe had 2670 planes, but more bombers than fighters. The RAF had 600 planes, but had radar which could give an early warning of enemy planes.

The battle began on 15 August 1940. For nearly a month the skies of southern England were full of twisting and turning fighter planes. By the beginning of September the RAF was running short of planes and of pilots. But the Germans were losing planes too. Suddenly the raids stopped. Hitler decided to use his bombers to bomb British cities. He expected this would make the British people so fed up that they would persuade their government to agree to stop fighting the Germans. But he was wrong.

The Blitz

From September 1940 to May 1941 German planes came at night to bomb London and other big cities. Clear moonlit nights were the worst because the Germans could see their targets easily.

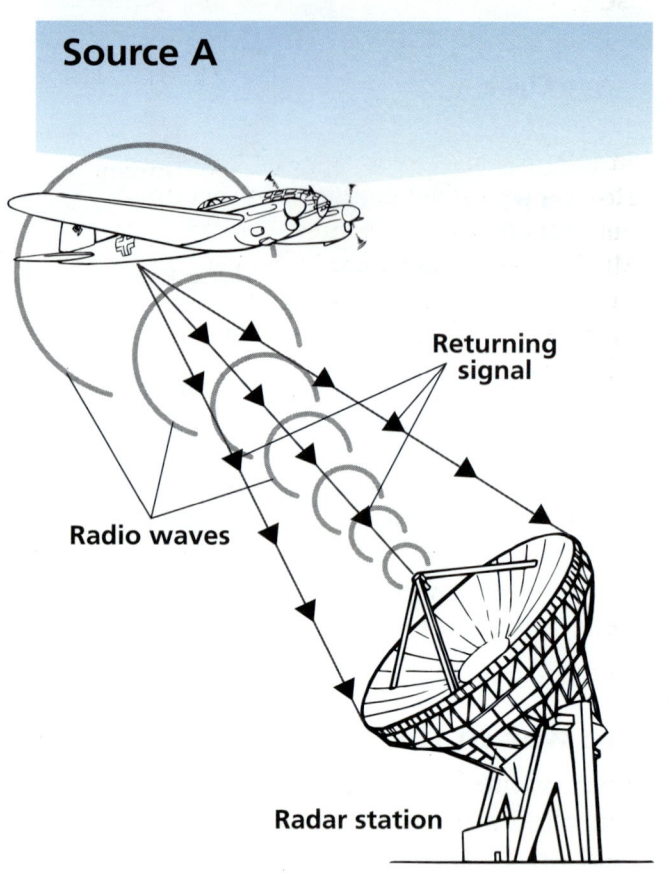

Source A

Returning signal

Radio waves

Radar station

Members of the WAAF (Women's Auxiliary Airforce) raising a barrage balloon. These balloons were held to the ground by cables. If bombers flew too low, they got caught up in the balloons or cables.

Source B

Source C

The first day of the Blitz from a report by Mass Observation.

At 8.15 pm a colossal crash, as if the whole street is collapsing; the shelter is shaking. A nurse begins to sing to drown out the noise. Mrs S. screams, 'My house! It hit my house!' As the bombing continues, a man shouts at the nurse who is still trying to get people to sing, 'Shut your bleedin' row.'

Sheltering

People sheltered from the bombs. There were dugout shelters in gardens (Anderson shelters). There were steel tables for the house (Morrison shelters). There were brick shelters in towns. Many Londoners slept in the Underground. Some people slept in their homes under the stairs (the strongest place in the house). Some people trekked out of the city every night to sleep in the fields.

Sirens and firewatching

When the bombers were spotted, a siren wailed to tell people to take shelter. Sometimes the raids went on all night. Fires broke out and the emergency services were at full stretch all the time.

Source D

This photograph was taken in London during the Blitz.

Questions

1. a When did the Battle of Britain start?
   b Why was it fought?
   c What did Hitler decide to do instead of continuing with the Battle of Britain?

2. Make a list of all the ways that people sheltered from the bombs. What would you choose to do?

3. Look at **Source D**.
   Some people think this photograph is posed so that it could be used for propaganda.
   a What clues are there that it might be posed?
   b How do you think the photograph might be used for propaganda?

2.4 BOMBS, BOMBS, BOMBS

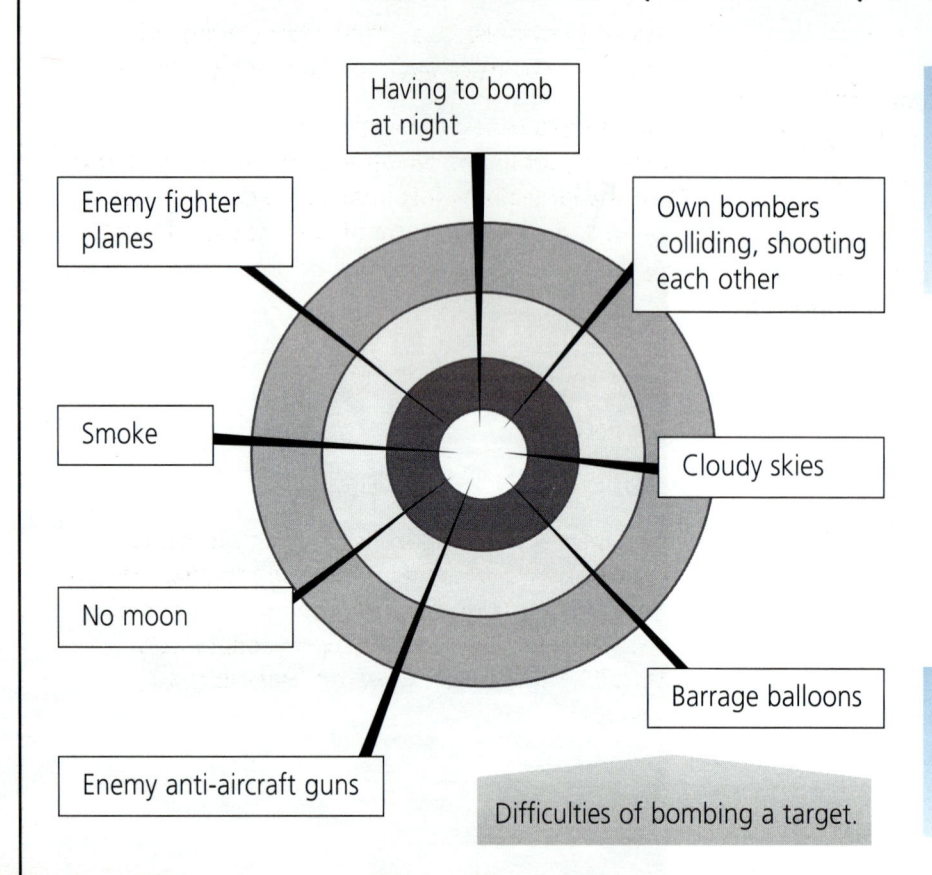

Difficulties of bombing a target:
- Having to bomb at night
- Enemy fighter planes
- Own bombers colliding, shooting each other
- Smoke
- Cloudy skies
- No moon
- Barrage balloons
- Enemy anti-aircraft guns

Source B
Bombs dropped on Britain and Germany, 1940–5.

Year	Britain	Germany
1940	37,000	10,000
1941	21,000	30,000
1942	3000	40,000
1943	9000	120,000
1944	2000	650,000
1945	750	500,000

Source C
Written by Vera Brittain in 1943.

The bombing of whole areas with their churches, libraries, schools, hospitals, museums and human beings came with the appointment of Sir Arthur Harris to the control of Bomber Command on 3 March 1942.

This is a policy of murder in the name of the British people.

Source A

"By the way, did you remember to feed the canary?"

This cartoon was published during the Second World War.

134

Why bomb?

Both sides used bombs to destroy factories, docks, railways and shipyards, and to frighten people so much they would surrender.

It was very difficult to bomb a target accurately. Wholesale bombing of cities became more and more common. Many people argued that this was total war. You could not make a difference between soldiers and civilians. By 1945 the airforce leaders of Britain and the USA argued that they could bring the war to a quicker end by massive bombing of German cities. They bombed the city of Dresden.

Dresden after the bombing in 1945.

Source D

Source E

Sir Arthur Harris, head of Bomber Command, explains why he ordered the bombing of Dresden.

Dresden had become the main centre for communications for the defence of Germany. It was also the largest city left intact; it had never been bombed. As a large centre of war industry it was important.

Source F

A German radio broadcast.

The Americans have proved they can hit precise targets. It would have been possible to spare the residential parts of Dresden. The use of firebombs proves that residential parts were deliberately attacked. It is pointless to drop firebombs on railways.

Questions

1. Look at **Difficulties of bombing a target**.
   a Which difficulties made bombers fly higher?
   b What difficulties did not go away even if the bombers flew higher?
   c Why do you think bombers flying to bomb their targets were so easily shot down by enemy fighter planes in daylight? Think of two reasons.

2. Read **Source E**.
   a What were the reasons Sir Arthur Harris gave for bombing Dresden?
   b Which reason do you think is the most important?

3. Read **Source F**.
   a According to the writer, what proves that residential parts were deliberately bombed?
   b Why do you think it is pointless to drop firebombs on railways?

4. Do you think that Britain and the USA were justified in bombing Dresden? Give reasons for your answer.

2.5 KEEPING THE CHILDREN SAFE?

What was evacuation?

Everyone was afraid that the cities would be bombed. The British government decided to send children to the countryside. They would be safer there.

1 September 1939

This was the start. Within a week the government had moved over a million children from cities to the country by train. About another million children were sent by their parents to live with aunts, grandparents and so on, far from cities.

How did evacuation work?

Children often went with the rest of their class at school. Often the teacher went too. The children were allowed one small case and a gas mask. They had a label tied to their coat giving their name and home address. Often parents did not know where their children were going.

In the country

Children stayed with families in the country. The government paid 10s 6d (53p) for the first child and 8s 6d (43p) for other children. Some children settled in well. Some were very unhappy.

Home for Christmas

By Christmas no bombs had fallen on the cities. Most children went home. When the bombs came a year later, some children were evacuated but most families did not want to be split up again.

Source A

Children walking to a railway station in London to be evacuated.

Source B

Beryl Hewitson remembers what happened when she arrived in the country.

We were told to sit quietly on the floor while villagers and farmers' wives came to choose which children they wanted. At last only my friend Nancy and myself were left. A large, happy-looking lady rushed in asking, 'Is that all you have left?' A sad nod from our teacher. 'I'll take the poor bairns.' We were taken to a farm where we spent two years.

Source C

Patricia Barton remembers being an evacuee.

It was gang warfare between us and the local kids. There wasn't a fruit tree within miles with a single item of fruit left on it. After a while things settled down to an uneasy truce.

Source D

Taken from reports to the Women's Institute in 1940.

We had never seen so many children with lice and nits. It seemed they hadn't bathed for months; some children had dirty sores all over their bodies. Some of the children were sewn into their ragged clothes. There was hardly a child with a whole pair of shoes. Many of the mothers and children were bedwetters and were not used to doing anything else.

Source E

Chris Portinari was badly bullied by two boys at one home.

They would tie me to a chair and hold red-hot pokers in front of my eyes. I had terrible nightmares. I was sent away when the three of us took down the knickers of the girl next door. I ended up in a spick-and-span place. I had to clean all the time. I saved my milk money, a halfpenny a day. I came home one day and wrote across the list of things I had to do, GONE BACK TO LONDON. My mother hid me for two days before telling my father. I wasn't sent back.

Source F

Some people looked after many evacuee children. They were sometimes given the British Empire Medal for this work.

Source G

Sheila Price was the second of eight children. She was twelve years old when she was evacuated.

We had a car to take us to school, a beautiful home, servants. Most of all we met with warmth and understanding.

Each weekend I'd go home. The street looked dingy and poor – I hated it. I remember seeing my father cooking a pigeon on our kitchen fire. Eventually Mother called me home to look after the others. Then my lovely world crumbled.

Questions

1 How would you have persuaded parents that it was a good thing to send away their children?

2 Read **Source B**.
When the children got off the train in the country, they usually went to the village hall. Country people who had room in their houses had been told they must take evacuee children. They chose the children they wanted. Often farmers chose strong boys to work on the farm. Other people chose clean children or pretty children or happy-looking children.
  a Why did the woman choose Beryl and Nancy?
  b Do you think they had a happy time with her?
  c Do you think children should have been chosen this way?
  d Can you think of a better way of organising which children went with which adults?

2.6 WINNIE'S WAR

Winnie married Leslie Williams in 1938. When war was declared in 1939 Leslie volunteered to join the Royal Engineers. In 1941 he was sent to Africa and then to the Middle East. He did not see his daughter until she was four years old.

Here Winnie remembers the war.

Keeping in touch

I never really knew where Leslie was, but sometimes he would write that he had had some leave in Alexandria or Gaza so I knew he was in the Middle East.

I sent him parcels. He always wanted Keatings Powders to kill lice and bed bugs. He always wanted soap too, especially shaving soap. Everything took such a long time. It was three weeks before he got the news that Margaret had been born.

A photograph of Leslie, taken during the war.

Source A

Air raids and eiderdowns

When the sirens went I would take the baby into bed with me and pull the eiderdown over both of us. A woman army officer was living with us. She used to come under the eiderdown too!

Fish and blackcurrants

Fish wasn't rationed, but there was very little. I queued for hours to get some for Margaret. Then she would only eat it if it was covered with blackcurrant purée.

War work

Before Margaret was born I worked in Chichester as a nurse with the VADs [Voluntary Aid Detachment]. I nursed soldiers and civilians.

In 1940, after Dunkirk, we all thought Hitler was going to invade and the south coast was a dangerous place to be. The civilian patients were all taken somewhere safer. For some reason I wasn't thought good enough to nurse soldiers, so I was sent to nurse people who were mentally disturbed.

Air raids and shelters

We had a spaniel who came with us when we visited my parents in Croydon. If there was an air raid he was the first by the shelter door. He was always the first out of the shelter when the 'All Clear' sounded.

Butter

Butter was rationed – sometimes only 2 oz (60 grams) a week. I used to pour the top of the milk into a small jar. Then I shook it until it turned to butter.

Children's parties

My friend was upset because she hadn't any eggs for her son's birthday cake. I made it for her; I used liquid paraffin. It worked beautifully.

A woman we knew asked us to bring our children to a party. There were scones thick with butter, iced cakes and chocolate biscuits. She must have got it on the **black market**.

A photograph of Winnie and Margaret, taken during the war.

Source B

Sausages and ham

We were only allowed 4 oz (113 grams) of meat a week, but sausages, when you could get them, weren't rationed. Our butcher sold sausage sandwiches. He put a slice of sausage meat between two slices of potato and dipped it in dried milk and breadcrumbs.

If I got a ham bone, I shaved the ham off and cooked it with potatoes and herbs. I boiled the bone up to make soup.

Eggs and hens

Eggs were rationed to one a week at the most. An old lady nearby kept hens and used to let me have eggs for Margaret. Then the men from the ministry stopped her. So she gave me two hens which she said had stopped laying. But they laid two eggs a day for me all through the war.

Questions

1. Why was it difficult to keep in touch with men fighting overseas during the war?

2. **a** What did it mean to have rationing?
   b What things did Winnie mention were rationed?
   c What things does she say were not rationed but were often difficult to get?
   d Why was food rationed during the war?

3. What does Winnie's account of the war tell us that history books don't?

2.7 THE SECRET ARMIES: THE RESISTANCE MOVEMENTS IN OCCUPIED EUROPE

Control by Germany
By 1942 Hitler controlled most of Europe. (Look at the map on page 128). These countries were occupied by the German army.

The choices
People living in these occupied countries had three choices.

- They could collaborate with the Germans.
- They could resist the Germans.
- They could get on with their lives as best they could.

The French Resistance
The Maquis was a famous French resistance group. It was made up of milkmen, plumbers, teachers, children and mayors, all working against the Germans.

What the Maquis did
The Maquis hid and helped Allied airmen who had been shot down. They blew up bridges and railways. By 1944 they were openly fighting the Germans. They sent reports to Britain to help with the D-Day landings.

What happened if they were caught?
The resistance fighters could be tortured to give the names of other resistance fighters. They were often killed. Sometimes the Germans punished whole villages. This was to set an example.

Source A
From a book called *The Maquis*, published in 1945.

We needed petrol. One night the Germans parked a tanker beside a wall of a building that was not guarded. A stonemason silently cut a hole in the wall. His comrades ran a pipe through to the tanker and all night pumped out the petrol. The stonemason rebuilt the wall. They did the same thing the next night. Before the Germans noticed, they put 200 kilos of sugar in the tank.

Source B

Danish resistance workers are listening to a radio broadcast from London in 1945. If the Nazis had caught them, they would have been killed.

The BBC broadcast news of the war which was different from the German version. They also broadcast coded messages for resistance workers in different countries.

The Netherlands

There were many people in the Dutch resistance. They ran an underground newspaper. This kept people in touch and made them feel better. Some worked against the Germans by blowing up German army vehicles. Some even assassinated leading members of the Nazi Party.

Hiding people

The Germans rounded up many Dutch people and forced them to go and work in Germany. The resistance managed to hide 300,000 Dutch workers who ran away. They also helped to hide Dutch Jews.

Source C

Anne Frank and her family were Jewish. In 1942 they and four others went into hiding. Friends kept supplying them with food.

11 July 1942: We've forbidden Margot to cough at night, even though she has a bad cold.

24 December 1943: Whenever someone comes in from outside, with the wind in their clothes and cold on their cheeks, I feel like burying my head under the blankets to keep from thinking 'When will we be allowed to breathe fresh air again?'

3 April 1944: The high point is our weekly slice of liver sausage, and jam on unbuttered bread. But we're still alive!

21 July 1944: Great news! An assassination attempt has been made on Hitler's life.

Someone tipped off the Gestapo. In August 1944 the family was arrested and sent to concentration camps. Anne's mother died in Auschwitz in January 1945. Anne and her sister Margot died of typhus sometime in February or March in Belsen. The Allies liberated Belsen in April. Anne's father survived until 1980.

Source D

There were large resistance groups in the German-occupied Soviet Union. These resistance workers are being hanged by the Germans.

Questions

1. What three choices did you have if you lived in an occupied country?

2. Read **Source A**.
   a. Was putting the sugar in the petrol tanker going to harm the German war effort a great deal?
   b. What sort of thing might resistance groups do that would harm the German war effort a lot?

3. Look at **Source B**.
   Why do you think some people in occupied countries risked their lives to listen to the BBC news?

4. Look at **Source D**.
   Why do you think the Germans punished resistance so severely?

2.8 THE SECRET ARMIES: THE SPECIAL OPERATIONS EXECUTIVE

Britain and the resistance groups

The only people still fighting Germany in 1940 were the British and the resistance groups in occupied countries. Britain set up the Special Operations Executive to work with resistance groups to bring down the Germans.

How they got there

The British recruited secret agents in Britain. Then they parachuted them into occupied countries. At first these agents often helped to set up local resistance groups. Later they worked with them.

Where they went

SOE agents went to many places:

- Yugoslavia
- Italy
- Norway
- Netherlands
- Belgium
- France.

Most of the agents went to France. France was very important because if Britain and other countries were ever going to attack Germany, they would probably have to land in France first.

Source A

Equipment to be dropped by parachute for the Maquis.

Source B

The head of SOE wrote:

All contacts with occupied countries closed when the last British soldiers returned to Britain in 1940. So the first man to go back to any country had to be parachuted 'blind'. There was no one waiting to help him.

Source C

A plane dropping SOE agents and equipment.

VIOLETTE SZABO

Violette's father was an English soldier who met and married her mother in France at the end of the First World War. Violette married a Free French soldier. She spoke perfect French and was adventurous. She joined the SOE and was parachuted into France many times.

Violette's last mission

It was 1944, just before D-Day. Violette was parachuted into France to take charge of a Maquis group. Things went wrong. Violette and the local Maquis leader were ambushed by German soldiers. Violette was injured and told the Maquis leader to get away.

She took cover behind some trees and held off 400 Germans and two tanks for two hours. Then she ran out of ammunition. She was captured and taken to Paris, then to Ravensbruck, which was an enormous concentration camp for women. She was shot there in January 1945.

HARRY RÉE

Harry Rée was a schoolteacher. He joined the SOE and was parachuted into France many times. He was never caught. This is one of his missions.

Peugeot made cars, but during the war the Germans forced the company to make parts for tanks and gun carriers. The RAF had bombed the works but done little damage. Harry was asked to blow up the Peugeot factory.

Captain Harry Rée.

The personnel manager secretly supported the resistance. He got Harry in to meet Monsieur Peugeot – the boss. Monsieur Peugeot gave Harry the plans of the factory and introduced him to two foremen who would help.

Harry arranged for explosives to be smuggled in and hidden in a cleaner's cupboard. The foremen placed the explosives and got out. At ten minutes past midnight the factory blew up. No one was caught.

Questions

1 Who were still fighting the Germans in 1940?

2 What countries did the SOE agents go to?

3 a If you were recruiting for the SOE, what sort of person would you select? Think of at least two skills they must have.
  b What things should SOE agents be trained to do?

4 Look at **Source A** and **Source C**. What sort of difficulties faced members of resistance groups when the RAF was making a 'drop'?

2.9 COLLABORATORS AND TRAITORS

Living in an occupied country

Most people tried to get on with their everyday lives. Things were very different with the Germans in charge.

Changes

- Factories were taken over to make things for the German war effort.
- Thousands of workers were sent to Germany to work for the German war effort.
- Banks were taken over by the Germans, so German gold reserves grew.
- German soldiers patrolled the streets.

Collaborators

Some people collaborated or worked to help the Germans. They paid a heavy price in the end.

Source A

This French woman was friendly with the Germans during the war. Now she is set upon by the people where she lives.

VIDKUN QUISLING (1887–1945)

Quisling founded a National Party in Norway in the 1930s. It was like Hitler's Nazi Party. In 1940 the Germans overran and occupied Norway. The king fled to Britain.

Quisling stayed in Norway. The Germans banned all political parties except the National Party. Quisling became prime minister. He ran Norway just as the Germans wanted it run.

When the war ended in 1945, Quisling gave himself up. At his trial it came out that he had been in contact with the Germans before the war. He had urged them to invade Norway. He was shot as a traitor.

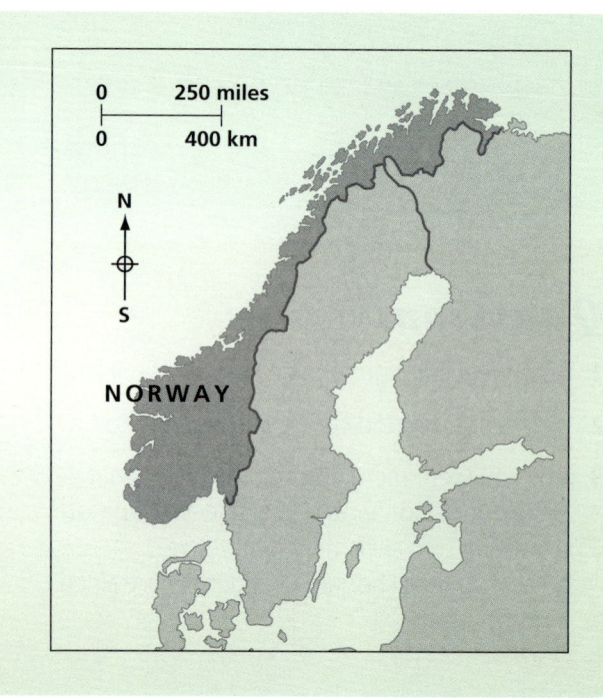

WILLIAM JOYCE (1906–46)

Joyce was Irish and came to England when he was sixteen. He joined the British Union of Fascists. Then he fled to Germany before war broke out.

For the whole war, Joyce broadcast to the British from Radio Hamburg in Germany. He forecast that certain places would be bombed, or that certain ships would be sunk, and so on. Although he was often wrong, he could be upsetting. He said Britain couldn't win the war. He needled people about food rationing and whether the British government was telling the truth.

In the end people laughed about him and called him Lord Haw-Haw because of the way he spoke. He was caught by British soldiers in Germany at the end of the war. He was brought back to Britain, tried and hanged for treason.

HENRI PHILIPPE PÉTAIN (1856–1951)

Pétain was a French soldier who became Commander-in-Chief of the French army in the First World War. Pétain was 84 at the beginning of the war. The French government asked for his advice. Once the Germans had invaded France, Pétain said the government should give up. The Germans divided France into two. Pétain ruled the southern half from the city of Vichy. He ruled it just the way the Germans wanted it. He did away with trade unions. He allowed only one political party. He had an anti-Jewish policy. At the end of the war he was tried for treason and put in prison. He was not executed because he was so old.

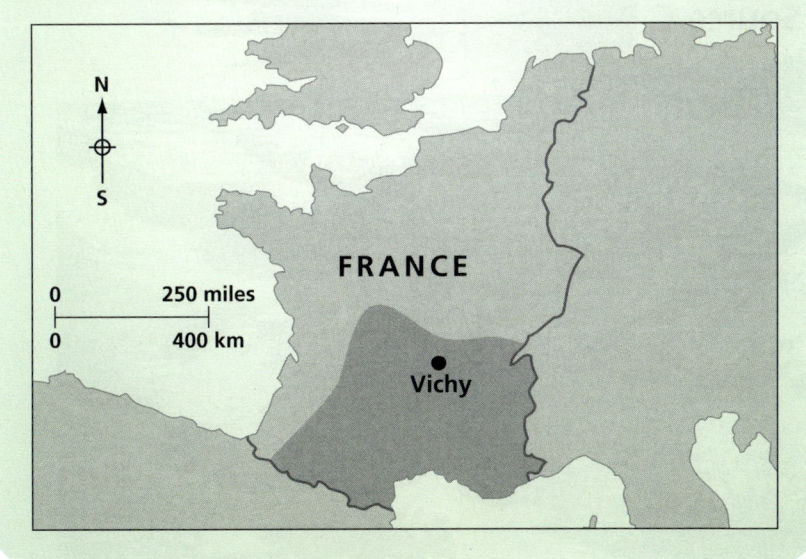

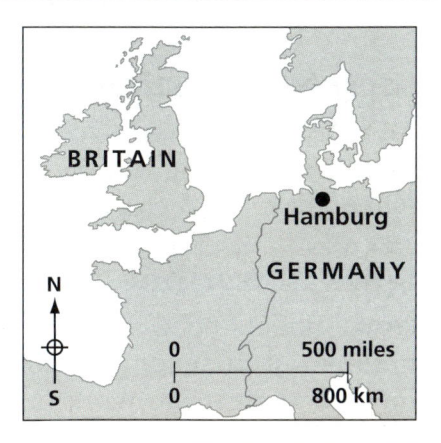

Questions

1 What were the changes that took place in occupied countries?

2 Look at **Source A**.
   a How is the woman being punished?
   b Why do you think she was not brought to a court of law?
   c Why do you think the woman might have been friendly with the Germans?

3 Read about **William Joyce**.
   a What was his nickname?
   b Where did he broadcast from?
   c How did he upset people?
   d Why do you think the British took a serious view of what he did?

2.10 SECRETS AND SPIES

Secrets in wartime
All governments keep secrets in wartime. This is to stop the enemy finding out plans for things like attacks or when ships will be in a certain place.

Spies in wartime
Governments need spies in wartime. They are needed for finding out the enemy's plans so that governments and military leaders can work out the best way to fight the war.

Source A

you never know who's listening!

CARELESS TALK COSTS LIVES

There were lots of posters warning people not to gossip.

Source B

Rescue workers are searching for survivors in a bombed school. The photograph was marked 'banned'.

Source C

This was to show people that expensive petrol was nothing to the hardships of the sailors who brought the petrol in ships. It was nearly banned in case it stopped men joining the navy.

"The price of petrol has been increased by one penny" – Official

The Enigma machine

Army commanders spoke to their officers by radio. They never knew if anyone was listening in. The Germans invented a code called 'Enigma'. It did two things:

- It 'scrambled' messages into code.
- It then adjusted the code minute by minute.

Breaking the code

A Polish worker passed details of Enigma to the British. Then the British set about breaking the code. Eventually they did it. But they did not let on they had broken it. That way they could go on listening into the German messages.

The man who never was

In 1943 the British dressed up a dead man in a Royal Marine's uniform and put false identity papers in his pockets. Then they chained a briefcase full of invasion plans to his wrist. They floated him in the sea off Spain. When the body was washed ashore, German agents got hold of the body and the briefcase. They had found the invasion plans for D-Day. But the British had completely misled them. The plans were for the wrong place.

RUDOLF ROSSLER

Rudolf Rossler was a German. When Hitler came to power he went to live in Switzerland. He joined a Russian spy ring and kept in contact with his German friends. Many of them became important officers in the German army and navy and the Nazi Party. Without knowing, they told him things about Germany's plans. He would then pass on the information to the Russians. For example, he warned the Russians that Germany was going to invade their country.

The spy ring was never broken.

Source D

An Enigma machine.

Questions

1. **a** Why do governments need secrets in wartime?
   b Why do governments need spies in wartime?

2. Look at **Source A**. Why did the artist draw Hitler and one of his supporters, Goering, behind the women on the bus?

3. Look at **Source B**. Why do you think the government did not allow this photograph to be published?

147

2.11 THE GIs: A DIFFERENT KIND OF INVASION

American soldiers come to Britain

The USA joined in the war in 1941 after the Japanese bombed Pearl Harbor. Soon there were plans to invade Europe so that the Allies could defeat Germany. This meant that hundreds of thousands of soldiers had to be gathered together for the invasion. The nearest jumping off place for Europe was Britain. So, from 1942 American soldiers were sent to Britain. By May 1944 there were over one-and-a-half million of them stationed in Britain.

The GIs

Ordinary American soldiers were called GIs. This was because their uniform was supposed to be stamped with General Issue. In fact their uniforms were very smart and light. Many British soldiers were envious. Their uniforms were thick, woollen and scratchy. But that wasn't the only cause for envy. A saying of the time was that there was nothing wrong with the Americans except that they were over-paid, over-fed, over-sexed and over-here.

Source A

Source B

A woman who was a teenager in the war remembers:

Americans were 'cheeky', but what a boost to the ego when one is greeted with 'Hello Duchess' (and you *were* treated like one). As we got to know these boys, how generous they were, we never lacked for chocolates or cigarettes or even luxuries like nylons that they could get for us.

The Americans were fun

Not everyone resented the American soldiers being in Britain. Britain had been at war for several years. Food was rationed. Clothes were rationed. Bombing, blackouts, difficult travel, long hours of work all made Britain a dull place. But the Americans were fun. They chewed gum. They danced. They had money. They had plenty of food and cigarettes. For many people, and especially young people, they were a breath of fresh air.

Non-combat soldiers

All these American soldiers had to be fed, paid, housed, have guns, tanks, aeroplanes and so on. The Americans had huge supply bases. By 1945 two of the biggest supply bases employed about 30,000 men. These men stayed there during the entire war. They spent their time off in local towns. They got to know local people.

Children stop an American serviceman to ask 'Have you any gum, chum?' They often did and gave it away to children freely. Sometimes gum was used as 'money' to pay for errands.

Source C

A GI remembers being invited home by a girl he met at a dance.

We had a meal which even by American standards was great. Only afterwards did I discover that I had eaten the family's rations for a month. So I went to see our Mess Sergeant and the next time I visited, I brought a large can of pears and a pork loin – and a lot more stuff.

British families were encouraged to entertain GIs. A rule was soon made that GIs took special rations with them, such as bacon, butter, coffee and sugar.

GI wives leave Britain for the USA in January 1946. This was the first ship they could go on because the American government used all ships to get their soldiers back first. 75,000 British women married GIs.

Source D

British girls dance with GIs at an American base.

Source E

Questions

1 a How many American soldiers were in Britain by 1944?
   b Why were so many American soldiers in Britain?
   c Why do you think there were so many GI brides by the end of the war?

2 Look at **Source E** and read the caption.
   a What do you think is going through the girls' minds – fear, regret, worry, excitement, hope, joy?
   b Why do you think they might have felt like this?

2.12 GERMANY – A DIVIDED NATION

D-Day
On 6 June 1944 the Allies invaded Normandy. All the long waiting and preparation was over. Hundreds of thousands of soldiers from Britain, America, Canada and many other countries leapt from landing craft and waded ashore to the beaches of France. Then they had to fight all the way to Germany. It took nearly a year. At the same time, the Russians were closing in on Germany from the east.

The end of the war
On 25 April 1945 Russian forces met with other Allied forces in the German capital, Berlin. On 7 May 1945 Germany surrendered. Hitler had committed suicide.

What to do about Germany
After the First World War, Germany had been forced to sign the harsh Treaty of Versailles. Most people realised that it had helped to cause the Second World War. They did not want this to happen again.

The biggest powers
The biggest powers were Britain, led by Winston Churchill, the USA, led by Franklin D. Roosevelt, and the Soviet Union, led by Joseph Stalin. They had met and talked about Germany even before the end of the war.

What the biggest powers agreed
- Germany should be divided into four. Each part would be run by a different power: the USA, the Soviet Union, Britain and France. Berlin would be divided in the same way. This was to be for a short time.

- The Allies would take goods and machinery from Germany to help pay for the war. The countries that had been liberated, such as Czechoslovakia, would be allowed to set up their own governments.

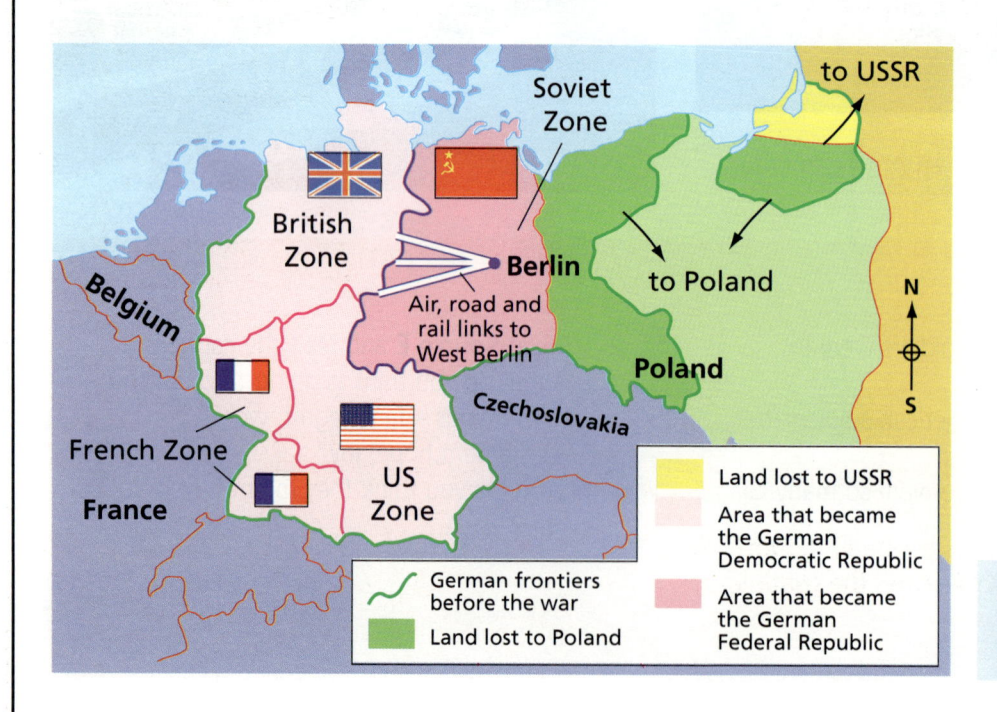

The division of Germany after the Second World War.

The Soviet Union and the small countries

The Soviet Union had been invaded by Germany. Perhaps as many as twenty million Russians had died. The Soviet Union did not want this to happen again. It decided that all the small countries next to it would form a buffer between the West and the Soviet Union.

The Iron Curtain

The Soviet Union forced countries such as Czechoslovakia and Hungary to have communist governments. They came under the control of the Soviet Union. Winston Churchill said that an Iron Curtain had descended across Europe.

Dividing Germany

In 1949 the British, American and French parts of Germany joined together to form West Germany. The Soviet Union's part became East Germany.

The Berlin Wall

In 1961 the Soviet Union built the Berlin Wall so that no one could cross from East Berlin to West Berlin. The Iron Curtain was well and truly down.

Source A

Part of a speech made by Winston Churchill in 1946.

From Stettin in the Baltic to Trieste in the Adriatic an Iron Curtain has descended across the continent.

Source B

A German soldier sits amongst the rubble of Berlin at the end of the war.

Questions

1.
   a. When was D-Day?
   b. How long did it take the Allies to force Germany to surrender after D-Day?
   c. The Allies advanced on Germany from the west. Which country advanced on Germany from the east?
   d. What happened to Hitler?

2.
   a. Why did the Soviet Union want to control the countries between itself and the West (particularly Germany)?
   b. Why did it want communist governments? (Think about what had happened in Russia in 1917.)

2.13 THE JAPANESE EMPIRE – A SHORT-LIVED SUCCESS

Pearl Harbor
The Japanese bombed Pearl Harbor on 7 December 1941. They did a lot of damage to the US navy. The Americans had to repair and rebuild ships.

The Japanese advance
The Japanese moved fast. The Americans had to rebuild their navy. The British, French and Dutch were busy fighting against Hitler. So the Japanese could take huge amounts of land in South-East Asia. No one was going to stop them.

Singapore
In six months the Japanese swept through South-East Asia. They took the British base in Singapore, and it looked as if they might attack India and Australia.

Asia for the Asians
The Japanese said they were liberating the countries in South-East Asia. These countries had been ruled by European powers. Now it was to be Asia for the Asians. But did the Japanese treat their fellow-Asians well?

Malaya
Malaya was one country taken over by the Japanese. The Japanese ran Malaya very strictly.

- Anyone resisting Japanese rule might be executed.
- The head of a family was punished if any member of the family misbehaved.
- All schools had to teach Japanese.
- Everyone had to sing the Japanese anthem.

What happened to Malaya?
The Japanese drove the British out. As they left, the British smashed up anything that might help the Japanese. This included bridges, railways and things to do with the tin and rubber industries. This led to more suffering for the Malayans.

The Japanese conquest of South-East Asia in 1941–2.

Questions
1. What were the four things the Japanese did to run Malaya strictly?
2. a What did the British do in Malaya as they left?
   b Why was this?
3. When the Japanese were defeated in 1945 what sort of rule do you think the Malayans wanted:
   a The British   b Independence
   c The Japanese? Explain your answer.

Source A

Japanese soldiers executing Malayan citizens.

Once the Japanese were in charge they took most of the medicines for the Japanese army. The Malayans were weakened from food shortages and easily died of illnesses like **malaria**.

It was difficult for the Malayans to see that the Japanese were any better than the British.

1942
By the middle of 1942, the Americans had rebuilt their navy. They won several naval battles.

The turning point
One famous battle was the Battle of the Coral Sea. However, the turning point was the Battle of Midway. The Americans lost ships but destroyed the Japanese aircraft carriers.

The importance of aircraft carriers
The Pacific Ocean was thousands of miles across. Aircraft carriers were vital. They were floating airfields.

The American advance
After the Battle of Midway, the Americans started to advance towards Japan. They captured one island after another.

Losses
Many of the islands were hard fought over. Both sides lost many men. The Japanese losses were greater.

1945
By the middle of 1945, the Americans were very close to Japan. The Japanese would not surrender. The next step was to invade the islands of Japan itself. But the Americans knew the Japanese would fight hard and many American soldiers would be killed.

To invade Japan or use the atomic bomb

As the Americans were winning the war with Japan, they demanded that the Japanese surrender fully. The Japanese would not surrender. The Americans had then to decide to invade Japan or use a new deadly secret weapon to destroy the Japanese will to fight on. They decided to use the new atomic bomb.

Enola Gay and the atomic bomb

It was 6 August 1945. The Enola Gay was a huge B-29 American bomber. Just after midnight it took off from the island of Iwo Jima. On board was the deadliest bomb ever made. It was so deadly that it was only finally put together after the plane had taken off. They flew over the Japanese city of Hiroshima at 8.15 am. Shortly after they dropped the bomb.

The city of Hiroshima had no warning. When the bomb exploded a brilliant light cut across the sky like a sheet of sun. The blast from the bomb knocked buildings down like toy bricks. More than 50,000 people died in less than a minute. Then the fires began.

Nagasaki

Still the Japanese would not surrender. So three days later the Americans dropped a second atomic bomb on Nagasaki. Then the Japanese surrendered.

Source B

A report to President Truman from some of the men who made the bomb.

We remind you of the report made to the late President Roosevelt in June 1940. It spoke of the danger of **radiation**. This bomb will kill men, women and children several miles around the explosion. They will go on dying after the bomb has fallen. This will be a completely new horror in war.

We began this bomb because we feared Hitler. Now Hitler is defeated and you want to use this terrible bomb against Japan. We believe this is wrong. America should not be the first to use this bomb. The saving of American lives would not make up for the horror and disgust against America for using it.

We recommend that one atomic bomb is dropped on an island where no one lives. This would give Japan a chance to see the power of the bomb and surrender.

Damage caused by the bomb at Nagasaki

Area of damage: 6.7 square kilometres
Houses completely destroyed or burned: 12,900
Houses badly damaged: 5509
Number killed: 73,884
Number injured: 74,909

Source C

Taken from reports by intelligence agents inside Japan, June 1945. Report made to President Truman.

Our agents all report an amazing will to fight on among the Japanese people. Our agents say that the Japanese people have been told by their government that the Americans plan to kill everyone in Japan. It is likely they will fight to the death.

Source D

Admiral Leahy speaking in 1950. He had been an adviser to President Truman in 1945.

In my opinion the Japanese were already defeated and were ready to surrender because of the effective sea blockade and the successful bombing with conventional weapons.

Source E

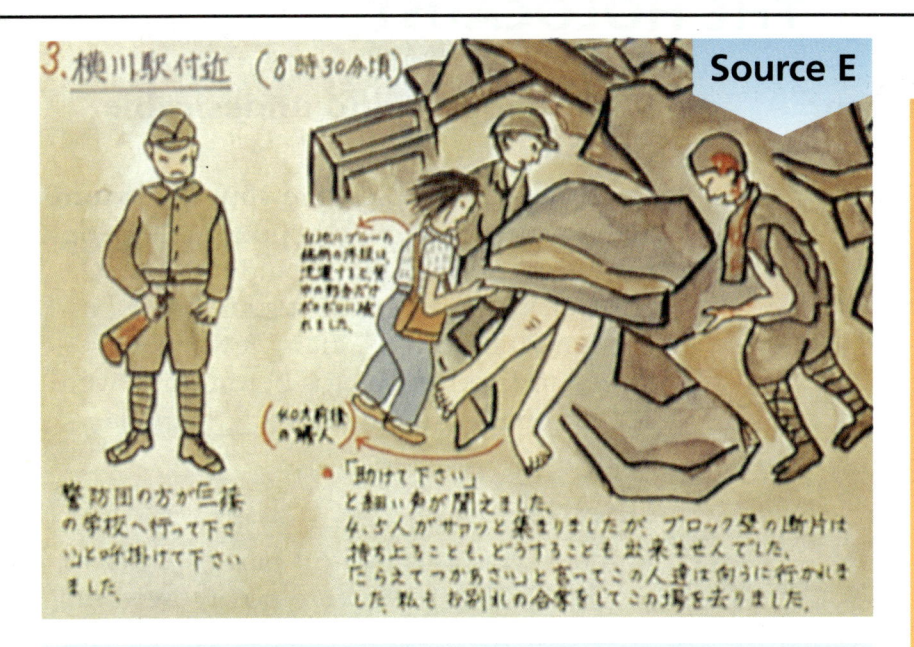

This was painted in 1975 by a survivor of Hiroshima. She saw this happen. The woman is asking for help. People cannot lift the concrete block off. The words say, 'Forgive us, the others left her as she was. I prayed for her and then left also.'

Source F

From a history book written in 1989.

After April 1945, what little shipping remained brought in coal and food. The war neared its end with Japan, not simply unable to defend itself, but realising that it could not feed itself into the next Spring.

Source G

From a history book written in 1989.

In six months in 1945, Japan was more heavily bombed than Germany was in the last three years of the war.

Source H

Hiroshima after the blast.

Questions

1 When was the bomb dropped on Hiroshima?

2 Read **Source D**.
   a Do any other sources support Source D? Which sources are they?
   b Do you think the writer of Source D might be biased? Explain your answer.
   c What would have happened to the Japanese if the Americans had gone on in the way that Admiral Leahy was suggesting?

3 If you had been President of the USA, would you have dropped the bomb on Hiroshima in 1945? Explain your answer.

2.14 THE HOLOCAUST

What does Holocaust mean?
Holocaust means wholesale destruction. Hitler wanted to destroy all the people he believed were undesirable. This was called the Final Solution and the Nazis devised several ways of achieving this, such as the setting up of ghettos and concentration camps.

Who were undesirable people?
- Jews.
- Handicapped people.
- Black people.
- Slavs (many East Europeans).
- Gypsies, communists and homosexuals.
- German people who spoke against Hitler.

Who were desirable people?
Hitler only wanted Aryans or pure Germans to live in Germany. A pure German was supposed to have blond hair and blue eyes.

What happened to undesirable people?
Handicapped people were shut in **asylums**. Many were killed. Some undesirable people were sterilised (so they could not have children). Many were sent straight to concentration camps. Many Jews were forced to lived in ghettos before they were sent to concentration camps.

Ghettos
A ghetto was a walled-off part of a city for Jews only. The Jews were not allowed out of the ghetto. They lived and worked there.

Concentration camps
A concentration camp was a large camp where thousands of people were herded together.

Removing those who starved to death in the Warsaw ghetto. The ghetto is behind the wall.

Source A

Perec worked as a weaver in the Lodz ghetto.

Source B

Esther and Perec Zylberberg

Six million Jews alone were killed by the Nazis between 1939 and 1945. Esther and Perec were two who survived. They lived in Lodz in Poland. The Nazis created a ghetto there in 1940. Perec was 16, Esther was 12.

Lodz ghetto

The ghetto was in a run down part of the city. There were about 30,000 one-room flats. 200,000 Jews were crammed into this ghetto. Only 700 flats had running water.

Soon some Jews were moved out. They were told they were going to be resettled on farmland outside Germany. They had to buy tickets and pack a bag.

ESTHER AND PEREC ZYLBERBERG

The Germans invaded Poland on 1 September 1939. They reached Lodz on 8 September.

Perec: *As we came to the city centre the first motorbike came into view. The thing that struck me was the clapping when they arrived. It was all those Germans who had been living in Poland as Poles. My mother said the Germans were hard but fair. A lot of people of her generation thought like that.*

Esther: *We were terrorised even before the ghetto was set up. I was very scared, but I also had a kind of childish excitement. The French and British were in the war now. The French had the best army and the British ruled the seas. The first painful thing was that my father had to flee. My brother David went too, to the Russian army. I never saw them again.*

The Chronicle

The Jews in the Lodz ghetto kept a secret diary called 'The Chronicle'. It tells us about conditions in the ghetto – how the Jews hoped the Nazis would soon be beaten or that they would treat the Jews better.

Questions

1 What does Holocaust mean?

2 What is a ghetto?

3 What were Jews told was going to happen when they were moved out of the Lodz ghetto?

Death in the ghettos and camps

Many people died in the ghettos from sickness, starvation or cold. But the Nazis wanted them to die more quickly.

Camps

The Nazis sent undesirable people to camps. There were three different sorts of camp.

- **Concentration camps.** These were prison camps. People usually died of sickness, starvation and overwork.
- **Labour camps.** These were large prison camps near factories where the prisoners worked. Again peopled died of sickness, starvation and overwork.
- **Death camps.** These were camps set up in 1941 for the sole purpose of killing people. This became known by the Nazis as the Final Solution.

> ### Source C
> From 'The Chronicle' of the Lodz ghetto. People suspected that those sent away went somewhere bad.
>
> Saturday, 15 July 1944: Today the Council Elder was told to halt resettlement. People hugged in the streets. No one thought whether this was a brief stop or a final stop to the sending away. The ghetto has lost the habit of thinking more than a few hours ahead.

Chelmno

The first Jews taken from the Lodz ghetto in 1942 were taken to Chelmno death camp. They were crammed into sealed vans and gassed with exhaust fumes. But this was not very efficient and used up petrol. In 1944 Chelmno was shut down.

Auschwitz and Birkenau

The next transports from Lodz went to Auschwitz. This camp had a death camp called Birkenau and a labour camp with factories. Hundreds of thousands of Jews died in the death camp. The Nazis found that the most efficient way to kill them was in gas chambers. The bodies were recycled by using the teeth, hair and so on, and even the ashes were used after the bodies were burnt.

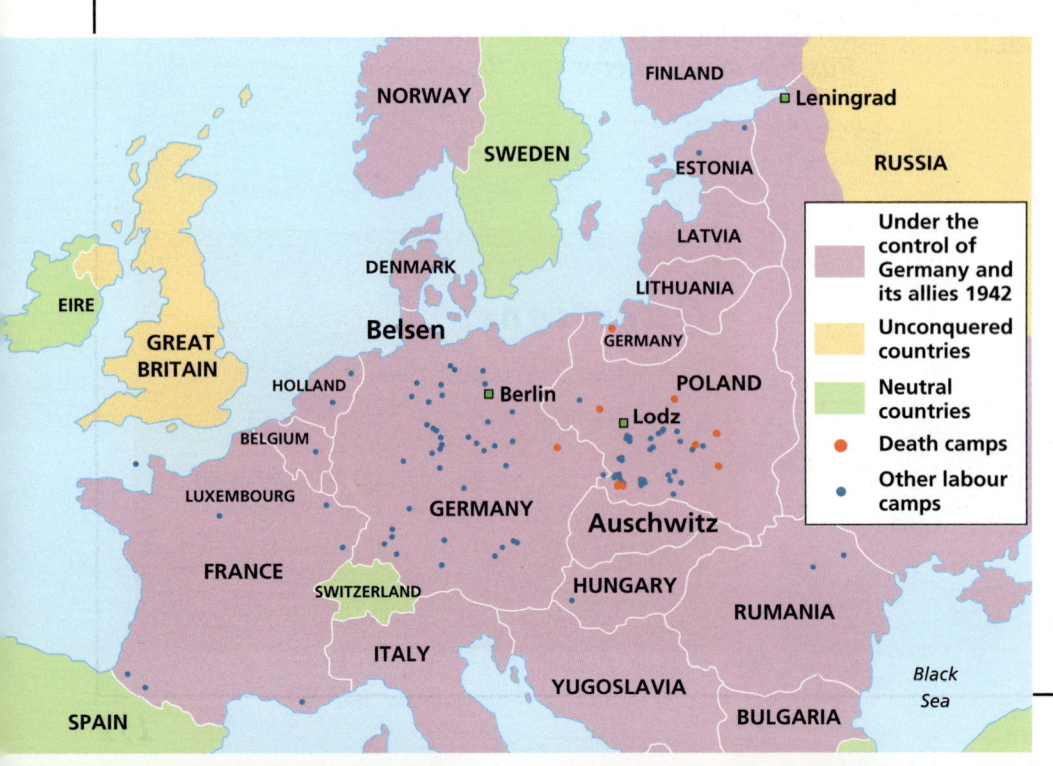

The Nazi camps.

Source D

The platform at Auschwitz where people were divided up. Some went to the labour camp. Some went to the death camp. This is what happened to Esther's mother.

Perec Zylberberg was 19 when he was transported to a labour camp at Czestochowa.

Perec: *I managed to get my mother and my sister into the carpet-making plant. We were starving, disease-ridden, in constant fear of almost everything.*

The work was hard. We hauled machine parts. The German guards carried whips but we were not beaten too often. It was a business-like slave organisation. There were Germans in charge, but they set up Jewish foremen and police. On 15 January 1945 we were woken early, given some bread and coffee and told to pack.

The Russians were close to Czestochow. Perec and other workers were marched deeper into Germany.

We were almost shoeless with no coats. The frosts were terrible. We had to clear the rubble when a nearby city was bombed. It was the first time I had seen ordinary Germans. Now and again a woman would give us a potato or a piece of bread.

Esther and her mother were sent to Auschwitz.

Esther: *All the people who were sent away from the ghetto were never heard of again.*

We had suffered hunger and disease for so long but we were not prepared for Auschwitz. When we arrived we said, 'Where are we?' The railway people said, 'You mean you don't know what this place is?' I had seen the barbed wire, people looking mad. We did not think we would stop there. They gave us a tin of food to eat while we were being pushed towards selection. This was the most painful moment, which I have never got over – separation from my mother.

Questions

1 What were the three types of camp?

2 What sort of things would stop the Jews being able to fight back against the Nazis?

3 What can we learn about the treatment of the Jews from the accounts of Esther and Perec Zylberberg?

The end of the war

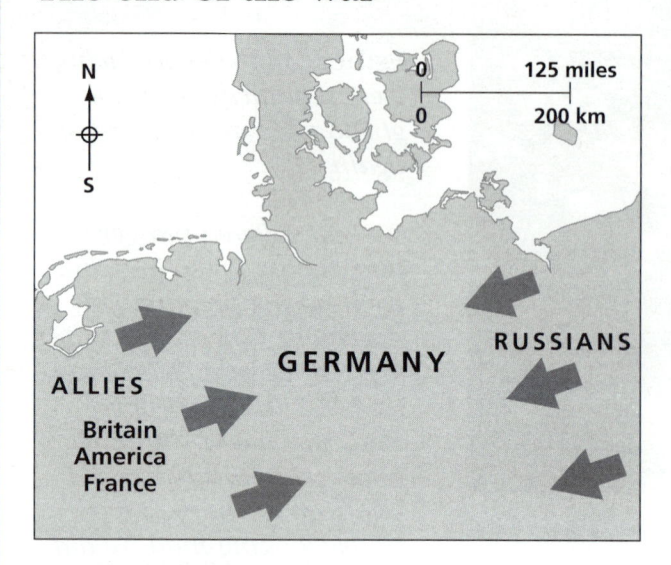

What happened?

As the Russians advanced on Germany, camps such as Auschwitz were closed. People were sent further into Germany. But the Allies were advancing from the other side too. Soon the camps were discovered. People were horrified.

Esther and Perec

Esther and Perec survived the camps but had to adjust to a new life. Survivors of the camps found this very difficult.

Source F

A British journalist wrote this account of Belsen. It was a labour camp. Esther had been marched there from Auschwitz.

Bodies in every state of decay were lying around, piled on top of each other.

One woman came up to a soldier and asked for milk for her baby. The soldier took the baby and saw it had been dead for days, black in the face and shrivelled up. She went on begging for milk. So he poured some on the dead lips. The mother carried the baby off, stumbled and fell dead after a few yards.

Everywhere there was the smell of death. Many people had typhus and dysentery. Most of the girls here are Jews from Auschwitz. Over and over I hear the same story of the parades where people were picked out for the gas chambers. To you at home, this is one camp. There are many more. This is what you are fighting. None of this is propaganda. It is the simple truth.

Source E

Just one of the hundreds of mass graves found by Allies in Nazi concentration camps.

Source G

Perec's family (before Esther was born). He was the only one to survive the Holocaust.

Esther and Perec were set free from the camps when it was clear that Germany was losing the war. These are what they said after they had left the camps.

Perec: *We passed through bombed out cities. It warmed our hearts. There is a sort of fog surrounding that journey in my memory. I seem to remember eating grass, leaves, bark. The trains went backwards and forwards and we lost count of the days and nights. Then we must have got somewhere. We got off. I heard about half the people had died, that some dead were eaten. I don't remember seeing that. Then I was in a building with bunks. There were nurses. I remember that. I remember being in a bed, clinging to a piece of bread. I had typhus and was in a clinic. The next thing I remember is a tank outside the window and thinking, 'the Allies are here'.*

Perec was one of 732 young people taken to England. They went to a hostel and then to homes all over England. Perec tried to find his family. Only Esther was found. Perec moved to Canada in 1958. He still lives there.

Esther: *Despite the fact that I knew what had happened to my mother, I had to keep on believing that somehow it wasn't true. I prayed, I don't know who to, probably myself, 'Please let me not be damaged for the whole of my life. Let me keep some love for people.'*

Esther came to England in 1947.

I lived with an elderly Jewish couple. They were kind but did not understand me. I longed to continue my education, to train as a nurse, but no one was prepared to give me my keep while I tried to replace my lost years.

Esther married another Holocaust survivor. They had two children. Esther now lives in London.

Questions

1 Why do you think survivors of the camps found it very difficult to adjust to a new life?

2 Read **Source F**.
What tells you that the journalist feels very strongly about what he has seen?

161

3.1 THE COLD WAR

The end of the Allies

The Second World War ended in 1945. Britain, the USA and the Soviet Union had been allies against Germany. But they did not stay allies for long. They were too different. Britain and the USA were capitalist countries (individual people owned farms, factories and so on). The Soviet Union was a communist country (the government owned farms, factories and so on).

The domino theory

The capitalist countries and the communist countries were afraid of each other. The USA and Britain were afraid that communism would spread from country to country like a disease. This was called the domino theory.

Buffer states

The Soviet Union had been invaded from the West several times. In 1919 the British, French and Americans had invaded the Soviet Union to help the anti-communists. Then in 1941, Hitler had invaded the Soviet Union. The Soviet Union wanted small, friendly countries between itself and the West (buffer states). The Russians had suffered very badly in the war. They never wanted to be invaded again.

The Cold War

The fear became so great that the next forty years of tension between the great powers were called the Cold War. Neither side went to war but it got very close.

Eastern European communist governments set up: Yugoslavia (1945), Bulgaria (1947), Poland, Czechoslovakia, Hungary, Romania (1948).

People's Republic of China, 1949
China became a communist country, helped by the Soviet Union.

The division of Germany, 1949
In 1949, Germany was divided into two countries:
- Communist East Germany allied with the Soviet Union.
- Capitalist West Germany allied with the West.

Czechoslovakia 1968, Poland 1981
These buffer states rebelled. The Soviet Union crushed the revolt.

The collapse of Eastern European communism, 1989
The Soviet Union began breaking apart because many people wanted change. In December, the USA and the Soviet Union said the Cold War was over. The Berlin Wall was pulled down.

NATO, 1949
The North Atlantic Treaty Organisation was an alliance of countries who said they would stick together against the Soviet Union.

Vietnam, 1959–75
The USA helped South Vietnam (capitalist) against North Vietnam (communist). In the end the USA gave up.

The Korean War, 1950–3
After the war the USA occupied South Korea. The Soviet Union occupied North Korea. They fought for three years then agreed to be two separate countries.

Cuba, 1962
Cuba became communist in 1959. Its leader, Fidel Castro, said the Soviet Union could build missile bases there. The USA was worried. The missiles could hit America. The USA threatened to attack the missile sites in Cuba. At the last minute the Soviet Union backed down.

The Warsaw Pact, 1955
This was an alliance between the Soviet Union and its buffer states.

The Berlin Wall, 1961
So many people wanted to escape from East Germany to West Germany that the Soviet Union built a wall to stop them.

Hungary, 1956
Hungary was a buffer state. It wanted more freedom from the Soviet Union. The Soviet army invaded the country and after five days of fighting, the Hungarian revolt was crushed.

Key:
- N.A.T.O. countries
- Warsaw Pact countries

Questions

1 What is the domino theory?

2 a What is a buffer state?
  b Look at the list below and at the writing round the map. Choose and write down the countries that were set up as Eastern European states (buffer states for the Soviet Union):
  China, Bulgaria, Britain, Argentina, Poland, Czechoslovakia, Yugoslavia, Belgium, Hungary, India, Malaya, Romania.

3 Look at an atlas. Which countries are likely to have joined NATO (North Atlantic Treaty Organisation)?

4 Why did the Soviet Union build the Berlin Wall?

3.2 THE CUBAN MISSILE CRISIS

Cuba became communist in 1959. The leader was Fidel Castro. The Soviet Union was on friendly terms with Cuba. This worried the USA. Cuba is on America's doorstep.

Soviet missile bases in Cuba

In October 1962, a US **reconnaissance** plane was flying high over Cuba. It spotted missile bases down below. They were Soviet bases. The USA was really worried. For the first time in history, the USA could be attacked by missiles (see map on opposite page).

What to do about the missile bases

John F. Kennedy was President of the USA. He called his advisers together. The question was what to do about the Soviet missile bases in Cuba. They talked for hours. On 22 October, President Kennedy ordered a naval blockade of Cuba. He wanted to show the Soviet Union that the USA was serious. The USA wanted the missiles out of Cuba.

Tense days

For several days it was very tense. It looked as if the USA and the Soviet Union might go to war over the missiles in Cuba. Then the Soviet Union backed down. A full nuclear war had been avoided.

Questions

1 Look at the box on page 165.
   a What were the three options that President Kennedy said they were talking about?
   b Read this page. What did Kennedy decide to do on 22 October?
   c Was this one of the options that they had talked about?
   d Why do you think they might have decided not to order the air strikes?

Source A

A photograph taken by a US reconnaissance plane in October 1962. The labels were put on by the Americans.

CUBAN CRISIS

All the discussions between Kennedy and his advisers about the Cuban missile crisis were taped. They were made public in 1997. This is from the tapes just after the US reconnaissance plane had taken photographs.

> **Who's who?**
> This list covers those people speaking in this extract. Others were involved in the debates.
> **Political advisers**: Robert Kennedy (the President's brother), Robert McNamarra (Secretary of Defense), Dean Rusk (Secretary of State).
> **Military advisers**: General Maxwell Taylor, Arthur Lundahl (an expert on interpreting photographs), Sidney Graybeal (a missile expert).

16 October Morning

Lundahl: *There's a missile launch site and two new army bases.*
Kennedy: *How do you know?*
Lundahl: *The length sir.*
Kennedy: *Is it ready to be fired?*
Graybeal: *No sir.*
Kennedy: *How long have we got?*
Graybeal: *If the equipment's checked sir, you're talking about a matter of hours.*
Rusk: *Do we assume these are nuclear?*
McNamarra: *There's no question about that.*
Rusk: *Sir, this is serious. We have to get rid of this base. We could make a quick strike – make it clear we were just wiping out the base. Or we can eliminate the whole island. Or we could take the political route. Make it clear we know what's going on. Demand to inspect the site.*
McNamarra: *If we're going to bomb these bases it has to be before they are armed.*
Kennedy: *So you're talking about:*
1 *Strike just the bases.*
2 *Strike the bases, airfields and anything else connected with the missile sites.*
3 *Do all that and blockade the island.*
There's the question of allied consultation. Don't think it'll be a lot of use. Probably ought to tell them though, night before.

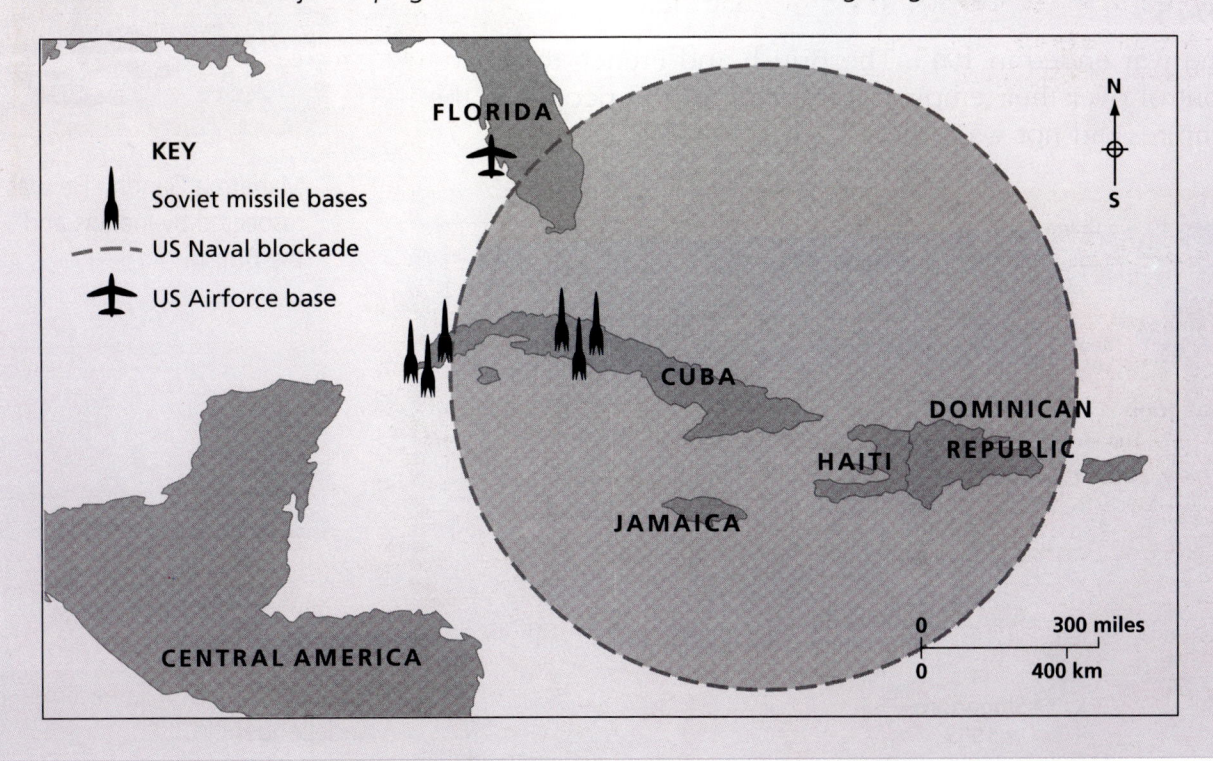

KEY
- Soviet missile bases
- US Naval blockade
- US Airforce base

FLORIDA
CUBA
HAITI
DOMINICAN REPUBLIC
JAMAICA
CENTRAL AMERICA

0 300 miles
0 400 km

3.3 EUROPEANS GO HOME

Spain, France and Britain
For hundreds of years Spain, France and Britain ruled large empires all over the world. By 1900, most of the countries in the Spanish Empire were independent. However, when the Second World War broke out in 1939, Britain and France still ruled large empires.

The Second World War, 1939–45
In 1940 in the war in Europe, France was defeated and Britain was fighting for survival.

In 1942 in the war in the Far East, Japan invaded and conquered countries in the British and French empires.

What did the people in the British and French empires think?
Until 1939, countries like Britain and France had seemed to be all-powerful. But suddenly in 1940 they were in trouble. This made people in their empires lose their fear and respect for them. In 1942, Britain and France were in even more trouble as the Japanese took land away from them in the Far East.

1945
The war ended in 1945. The British and French resumed control over their empires. But many of the people of the empires did not want them back.

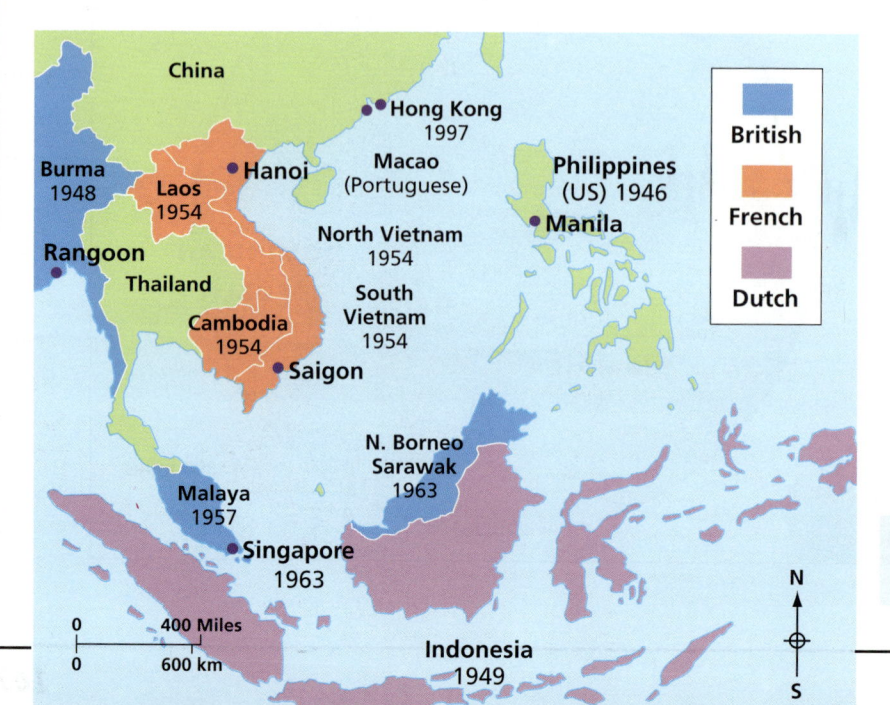

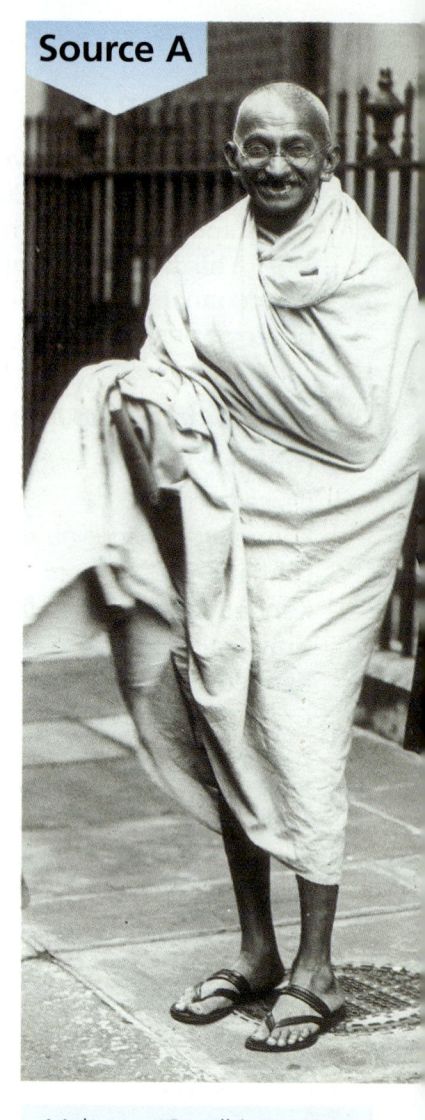

Source A

Mahatma Gandhi. He was respected by Indians and the British.

How South-East Asia became independent.

Britain and France were short of money

The war had cost a lot of money and after it Britain found it hard to pay to run an empire. A Labour government was elected in 1945 in Britain. It was happy to make India independent. This happened in 1947.

Education and nationalism

British and French rule had brought education to all the countries in their empires. This education led many of them to think about ruling themselves. There was more and more nationalism (the feeling of belonging to a particular country such as Britain or Kenya or India).

Nationalist leaders

Nationalist leaders appeared in many countries. There was Mahatma Gandhi in India, Kenyatta in Kenya and Nkrumah in Ghana. Many other countries fought for their independence too, such as Algeria and the Belgian Congo.

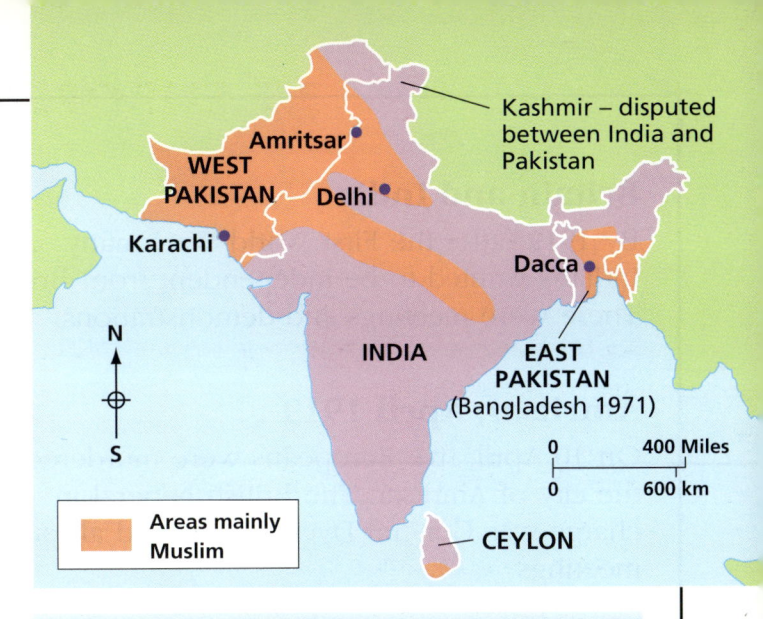

India after independence.

End of the empires

By 1970 all the European empires had gone. Only some very small islands that were not strong enough to stand on their own remained in the empires.

How Africa became independent.

Questions

1. What happened to France and Britain in 1940?
2. What did the Japanese do in 1942?
3. Give two reasons why the British and French empires came to an end after the Second World War.
4. What is nationalism?

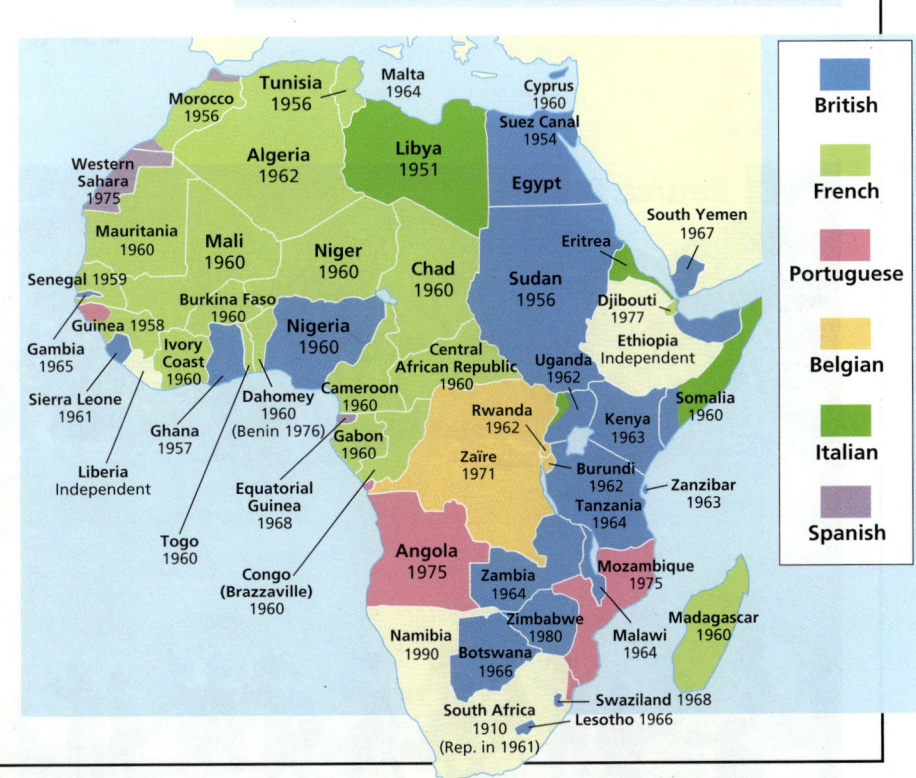

167

Britain and India

By 1919 (after the First World War) many Indians wanted to be independent from Britain. There were meetings and demonstrations.

Amritsar, April 1919

On 10 April, five Europeans were murdered in the city of Amritsar. The British general in charge was General Dyer. He banned all public meetings.

Defying the ban

A crowd of over 5000 Indians met in a part of Amritsar called Jallianwala Bagh. They wanted to listen to speeches criticising the British. General Dyer decided to break up the meeting.

The Amritsar Massacre, 13 April 1919

Jallianwala Bagh was surrounded by a high wall. Dyer told his soldiers to open fire without warning. About 2000 people, including women and children, died or were wounded. The British dismissed General Dyer from his command.

Source C

From *The Times*, 27 May 1920.

The government has said that although there were problems in the city, Dyer should not have punished an unarmed crowd which had done nothing violent. It had not tried to fight him and many of the crowd probably did not know of his ban on having meetings.

Source D

From the *Daily Mail*, 4 May 1920.

TINY LOYAL FORCE AGAINST GREAT CROWD OF INDIANS.

Despite this [General Dyer's orders], the Indians gathered in large numbers at Jallianwala Bagh -- estimates vary between 5000 and 30,000. Dyer, who was in command of a little force of less than a hundred soldiers and two armoured cars, gave the order to fire.

Source B

A scene from the film *Gandhi* showing Dyer's troops firing on the crowd.

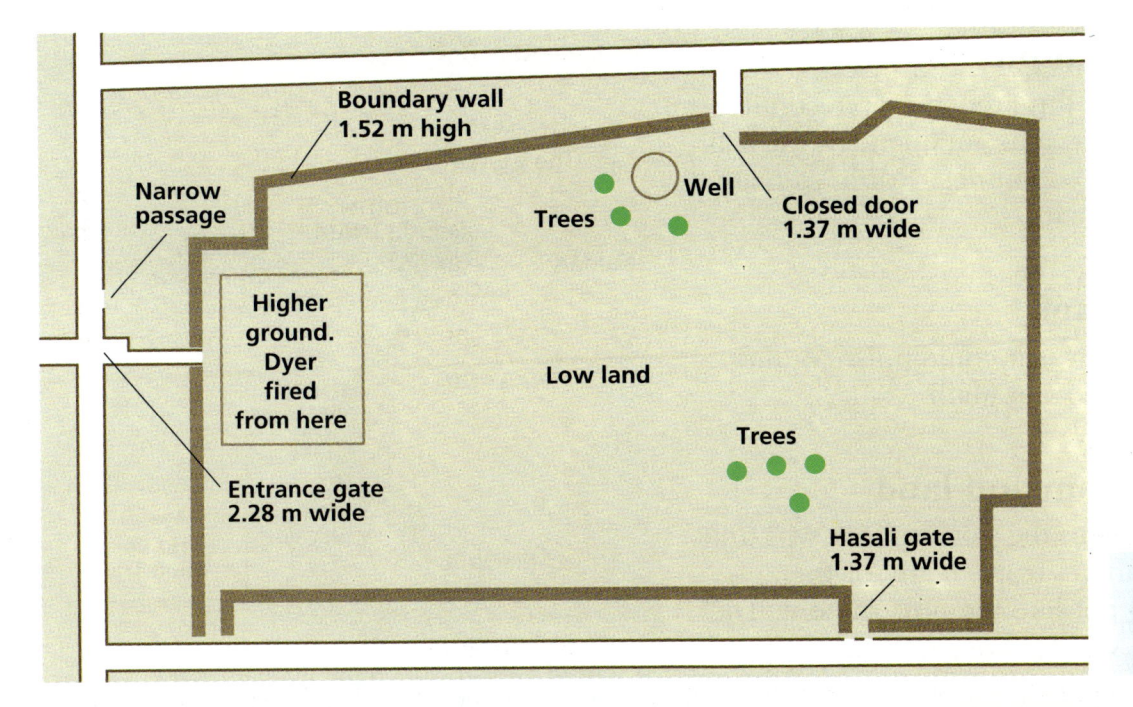

Map of Jallianwala Bagh.

(Map labels: Boundary wall 1.52 m high; Narrow passage; Trees; Well; Closed door 1.37 m wide; Higher ground. Dyer fired from here; Low land; Trees; Entrance gate 2.28 m wide; Hasali gate 1.37 m wide)

Source E

Part of an interview with General Dyer in the *Daily Mail*, 4 May 1920.

I had to shoot. I had thirty seconds to make up my mind about what to do. If I hadn't I, and my little force, would have been swept away. Then what would have happened?

Source F

Part of the evidence given by General Dyer to the Hunter Committee, set up to investigate the massacre.

Question: You did not issue a warning. Did you think you were going to be attacked?

Dyer: It was serious. It was not just dispersing the crowd. I had to have a show of strength not just for the area but for that part of India too.

Question: When did you decide to fire?

Dyer: When I first heard of the meeting.

Questions

1. What happened on 10 April 1919?
2. What did General Dyer decide to do?
3. How many people met at Jallianwala Bagh?
4. What happened at Jallianwala Bagh on 13 April 1919?
5. Do you think the British government was right to dismiss General Dyer? Support your answer using the sources.

3.4 THE WAR IN VIETNAM

The end of empire
Vietnam was in the French empire until 1954, when it became independent. It was made up of two countries: North Vietnam and South Vietnam.

North Vietnam
North Vietnam was a communist country. It was led by Ho Chi Minh.

South Vietnam and land
In South Vietnam the government was anti-communist and corrupt. Many of the peasants did not like the government. The main reason was because of who owned the land. There were 11 million peasants living around the mouth of the Mekong river. Two million had no land. The other 9 million paid high rents to landlords miles away.

The Vietcong
The Vietcong were communist rebels inside South Vietnam. In places where they had control they gave land to the peasants. This made them popular. The government did nothing to help the peasants.

South-East Asia during the Vietnam War.

The USA and communism
The USA did not want communism to spread in the world. They worked hard to stop it in Europe. Now they were afraid it would spread in the Far East. If South Vietnam fell to communism then other countries would follow like dominoes falling over. So the USA decided to support the government in South Vietnam despite the fact that many South Vietnamese did not.

The domino theory.

The Vietnam war

From 1955, the USA sent weapons and army advisers to South Vietnam to help the fight against the Vietcong. In 1963, the new American President, Lyndon Johnson, decided to send more help. By 1968 the USA was spending thirty thousand million dollars a year and 300 soldiers a week were dying.

Meanwhile North Vietnam was supplying arms to the Vietcong in the south. In turn, North Vietnam was helped by the communist countries of the Soviet Union and China.

What sort of war?

The USA had fantastic technology and lots of bombs. There was everything from helicopter gunships to electronic sensors. Usually the sensors were in planes and detected places like gun sites by means of infra-red image intensifying devices. Planes also carried sensors to detect radar missile signals. The best known, but not always the most effective sensor was the 'People Sniffer'. It was carried in helicopters. The sensor could detect human chemicals from sweat and breathing.

Guerrilla war

The Vietcong did not fight open battles. They raided and ambushed American soldiers and then disappeared into the jungle. This was frustrating for the Americans. Sometimes they took revenge on suspected Vietcong hideouts and killed innocent people. They bombed the Ho Chi Minh Trail to stop supplies coming from North Vietnam. They used chemicals to burn large areas of jungle.

More and more protests in the USA

Americans saw pictures of the war on television. They were more and more horrified. There were marches and protests against the war. In 1973, the Americans pulled out. Two years later North Vietnam invaded South Vietnam.

Source A

American soldiers on patrol encounter bamboo spikes laid by the Vietcong, as described in Source B.

Source B

A member of the Vietcong describes the best way to fight the Americans.

Let me tell you how we fought the Americans. We knew that we did not have the weapons to fight them in the open, so we had to fight another way. For instance, we would put sharp bamboo in the ground near the paths the Americans walked on. Then we would shoot. They jumped off the paths and got hurt on the bamboo.

Then the Americans always did the same things. They would be angry, they might kill some people, or shoot up some houses and so on. They never found us, but they made many enemies when they did these things.

My Lai Massacre, 1968

On 16 March 1968, 150 American soldiers and 5 officers landed by helicopter near the South Vietnamese village of My Lai.

The orders

The orders were to make sure the village had no members of the Vietcong in it. When the soldiers landed they were not shot at. They did not see any Vietcong.

The massacre

Lieutenant William Calley led his soldiers into the village. They rounded everyone up. Some of the women were raped, other people were gunned down. A group of old men, women and children were herded together and shot.

About 150 unarmed people were killed.

Source C

An account of the attack from a villager who survived.

Nothing was happening here. Then the helicopters came and the soldiers surrounded us. They were firing their guns and people were dying. I pushed my son into the paddy field and lay on top of him. Corpses fell on top of us. I told him, 'Don't cry and see if we can survive.' The people who were still alive were shot again and again. I hate the Americans. I shall never forgive them.

This photograph shows some of the dead at My Lai.

Source D

Source E

An army sergeant comments on the purpose of the attack.

The understanding, or the order that was given, was to kill everyone in that village. Those people, the women, the kids, the old men, were Vietcong or sympathetic to the Vietcong. It was quite clear that no one was to be spared.

Source H

An American soldier comments on the problems faced by the US army in Vietnam.

You had little kids in Vietnam who would shoot you in the back as you walked away. I couldn't work out which people were the enemy. All of them looked the same, North Vietnamese and South Vietnamese.

Source F

Said by Lieutenant Calley at his trial. He was the only one convicted for the massacre at My Lai. He was given a life sentence but released three days later.

My troops were being massacred in Vietnam by an enemy they could not see. The enemy was communism. When I came face to face with it, I had to put the lives of my own troops first.

Source G

Survivors of My Lai being comforted after the massacre.

Questions

1. **a** Who led the North Vietnamese?
   b Were the North Vietnamese communist or anti-communist?
   c Who helped the North Vietnamese when they went to war with the USA?

2. **a** Why did a lot of the South Vietnamese not like their government very much?
   b Who were the Vietcong?
   c Why was it likely that many South Vietnamese peasants would be sympathetic to the Vietcong?

3. Read **Source F**. Had Calley really come face to face with communism in My Lai? Explain your answer.

4. Killing women and children was obviously wrong. Why do you think these Americans did it?

3.5 THE UNITED NATIONS: AN ORGANISATION FOR PEACE?

The Second World War was horrific. So many died and so much was destroyed. People did not want such a war again.

The United Nations, 1945

The representatives of 50 countries met in San Francisco. They wanted to set up an organisation to keep world peace. It was to replace the League of Nations. What they agreed to set up was to be called the United Nations.

Source A

This is the way in which the United Nations was organised.

United Nations Secretary General

Runs the UN aided by officials from all the member states.

Security Council

- Takes day-to-day action on behalf of the General Assembly.
- 15 members – the five great powers (UK, USA, CIS, France, China) and ten other nations elected for two years at a time.
- All decisions have to be carried by nine members voting YES and none of the Great Powers voting NO (the veto).

General Assembly

The parliament of the United Nations.
- Each member state has one vote.
- Meets once a year in September.
- Special meetings can be held in an emergency.
- Important matters decided by a two-thirds majority; other decisions by a simple majority.

UN ORGANIZATIONS AND AGENCIES

Other organizations and agencies do much of the most valuable work of the UN, such as WHO (health) and UNESCO (education).

Source B

The United Nations Charter.

WE, THE PEOPLES OF THE UNITED NATIONS, ARE DETERMINED

- To save people in the future from the horrors of war which twice in our lifetime has brought untold sorrow.
- To reaffirm faith in human rights, in the dignity and worth of the human person, in the equal rights of men and women and of nations small and large.
- To have respect for international law.
- To encourage better standards of life.

A cartoon published in 1945.

Source C is

"A FINE TEAM — BUT COULD DO WITH A DASH OF UNITY...."

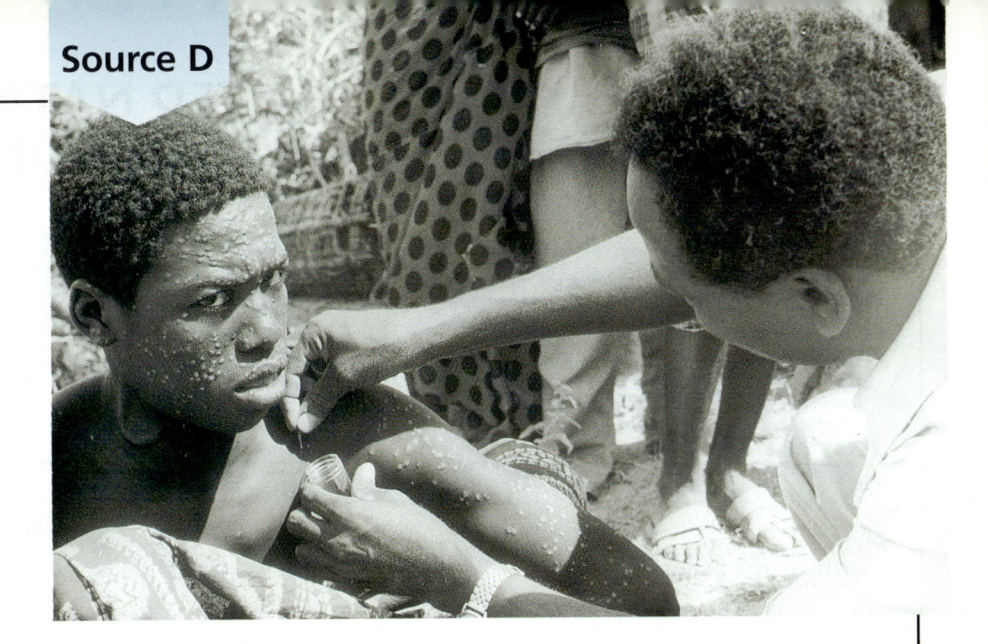

Source D

The WHO campaign to rid the world of smallpox, 1967.

What the United Nations did

The United Nations set up several different organisations to deal with certain problems in the world.

- The International Court of Justice deals with international arguments over territory and so on.
- The United Nations International Children's Emergency Fund looks after needy children in poor countries of the world.
- The World Health Organisation fights disease. One of its achievements was to help wipe out smallpox.
- The United Nations Educational, Social and Cultural Organisation helps to educate people throughout the world.

Source E

Learning to read in Morocco, 1960. Part of UNESCO's work.

Questions

1 Look at **Source B** (the United Nations Charter) and at **What the United Nations did**.
   a What are the aims of the United Nations (Source B)?
   b Which parts of the United Nations carry out these aims?
   c Which aim in Source B is not covered by a United Nations organisation mentioned on this page?
   d What would you do about the aim to save people in the future from the horrors of war?

2 What do you think **Source C** is trying to say?

3.6 THE UNITED NATIONS: AN ORGANISATION FOR WAR?

One of the aims of the United Nations was to keep peace. Keeping peace, however, often meant going to war!

Korea, 1950–3
UN soldiers (mostly from the USA) helped South Korea against communist North Korea.

Suez, 1956
British, French and Israeli soldiers invaded the area around the Suez Canal Zone. The UN forced them to leave.

Arab-Israeli conflict
From 1957 to 1967 UN soldiers patrolled the frontier between Israel and Egypt. When they left war broke out.

The Congo, 1960
The Congo became independent in 1960. Law and order broke down. The UN sent soldiers from Canada, India, Ireland, Ghana and Nigeria. UN doctors and other experts went to help too.

Did the UN always send in soldiers and help?
The UN did not do anything about the following:
- Hungarian rebellion against the Soviet Union (1956).
- The Cuban missile crisis (1962).
- The Vietnam War (1959–73).
- The Falklands War (1982).

Source A

HISTORY DOESN'T REPEAT ITSELF

The cartoonist compares the League of Nations and the United Nations. Unlike the League, the UN could use force.

Source B
Written in 1957 by the historian David Thomson.

The veto made the Security Council of the United Nations ineffective in taking action against the superpowers, the USA and the Soviet Union.

Part of Operation 'Desert Storm'. Katherine Jenerette is on the right.

Source C

Why didn't the UN always send soldiers or help?

There were usually two reasons. Either the main countries of the United Nations could not agree on what to do or the Great Powers ignored what the UN said.

The Gulf War

On 2 August 1990, Iraq invaded the tiny oil-rich state of Kuwait. The UN acted in certain ways.

- **2 August** – demanded Iraq's withdrawal.

- **9 August** – imposed **sanctions** on Iraq (no trade).

- **25 August** – threatened to send troops if necessary.

- **29 November** – insisted that Iraq must withdraw by 15 January 1991.

- **17 January** – sent 200,000 UN soldiers.

- **26 February** – liberated Kuwait.

- **5 April** – approved ceasefire.

KATHERINE JENERETTE

Katherine Jenerette took part in 'Desert Storm' (the Gulf War).

Desert Storm was exciting but at the same time in the back of my mind I thought, 'I could really die'.

I remember taking our gas masks everywhere – the bathroom, the shower, even when I was out jogging.

My adventures included black-out driving through the desert to find a telephone satellite site, dust storms, scuds overhead, keeping as much 5.56 ammo in my web gear as I could carry for my M-16 and, the hardest part, losing a friend killed by a land-mine.

What were we really fighting for? Us soldiers knew we were fighting to protect America's way of life – OIL. We were not there to spread democracy.

Questions

1. Read **Source B** and look back to the structure of the UN on page 174.
   a. What was the veto?
   b. Which country might have vetoed the UN going into Hungary in 1956?
   c. Which country might have vetoed the UN going into Vietnam? (You may need to look back to page 170).

2. Look at **Source A**.
   a. Do you think the UN needs to be able to send soldiers to stop war? Give one example from page 176 of the UN stopping a war.
   b. Did the UN ever fail to stop a war in the end? Give one example.
   c. Has the UN ever done nothing to stop a war or conflict? Give one example.

3. Read about **Katherine Jenerette**. What does she say the US soldiers were fighting for?

3.7 POSTWAR BRITAIN: EARLY CHILDHOOD MEMORIES 1947–52

This unit and Unit 3.8 are about memories. Memories are important. But they are not always accurate. In the following accounts, one is from personal experience, the other is from a historian's point of view.

● This is a personal memory of postwar Britain.

◇ This is a historian's account of what happened.

Bomb-sites

● Everywhere you went in London there were bomb sites. You could see the inside bits of houses with wallpaper and shelves still there.

◇ The government had lots of prefabricated small houses made. They were called 'prefabs'. This was to house bombed-out people. The long-term plan was to build new towns in the country.

The National Health Service

● One morning Dad went to see our doctor to ask about the new National Health Service. The doctor said, 'I didn't think you wanted that kind of service.' But we joined all the same.

◇ In 1946 the government passed the National Health Act. This provided free medical care. It was paid for by the taxes everyone paid.

The Festival of Britain

● My grandparents took me all over London. They wanted to take me to the Festival of Britain. But for some reason Mum and Dad wouldn't let me go and they wouldn't take me themselves.

◇ The Festival of Britain was held in London in 1951. It was to celebrate the new Britain after the war. Things were going to get better. There were fun fairs and exhibitions of things made in Britain, cafés and gardens.

Source A

The Halls of the Festival of Britain.

Source B

A British Restaurant.

Shopping and rationing

- I used to go shopping for my mother. This could take a morning, even though the shops were just round the corner. Most of the time was spent queuing – especially for bread and meat. One day word went round that a shop had 'viyella' material. My mother and her friends queued for hours. Then we all had clothes made of viyella for years.

- In 1946 there was a world wheat shortage. Bread was rationed, something that hadn't happened even in the worst days of the war. Gradually, however, rationing stopped. Chocolates, sweets, eggs and sugar came off ration in 1953. Coke, margarine, butter, cheese, meat and bacon came off in 1954. That was about the end of rationing.

Eating out

- Every week I went with my mother to a restaurant. It was by the railway bridge. We sat at wooden tables and the chairs were wooden and folded flat when they weren't used.

- British Restaurants provided good, cheap meals. They were started during the war. They helped a lot of people eat properly when food was rationed. The cost was subsidised by the government.

Fighting fathers?

- Friends laughed at me because during the war my Dad joined the Home Guard. My friend Gillian's father was a **dispatch rider** in Italy. That was terribly glamorous. When I went round to tea he cooked us marvellous spaghetti bolognese.

- The Local Defence Volunteeers (known as the Home Guard) were formed in 1940. About half a million men joined. Their job was to defend Britain if the Germans invaded. They were mostly older men or men waiting to join the army. Through the war they manned anti-aircraft guns and so on. They disbanded in 1944.

3.8 POSTWAR BRITAIN: SCHOOLGIRL MEMORIES 1952 ONWARDS

Changing schools

- *We took the 11-plus examination. This one exam decided which school you went to next. We all wanted to go to the best grammar school in our city. No one wanted to go to a secondary modern school. I was promised a bike if I passed and a tennis racquet if I didn't. But I found the bike hidden in our shed, so I knew I would get it anyway!*

- In 1944 Parliament passed an Education Act. It set up three types of secondary school:
  - Grammar
  - Modern
  - Technical

  Children were sent to the best school for them. In 1965 the Labour government said there must be a change to comprehensive schools. In 1970 the Conservative government said schools did not have to be comprehensive.

Capital punishment

- *In English lessons we often had debates. Someone would speak for something and someone else would speak against. After they had spoken anyone could join in. At the end we voted.*

  In 1955 Ruth Ellis was hanged for shooting her lover. She had discovered he was unfaithful to her. We debated the rights and wrongs of this. I made up my mind then and I haven't changed it since.

- In 1957 Parliament abolished hanging except for killing a police officer, killing whilst stealing or by shooting or by explosion. In 1969 the death penalty was abolished for good.

Equal opportunities

- *A careers' woman came to school. She said we could be anything from an airline pilot to a plumber. But then she went on: 'Whatever anyone says, the best jobs for women are nursing and teaching.' Our teachers were furious. They had been saying we could do anything. In one way they were right. But they never told us how difficult it was being a woman in a man's world.*

- From 1975 men and women were to be paid the same money for the same job or for a job of the same sort.

Source A

The Aldermaston March.

Divorce and pregnancy

- Two major things happened in my class when I was fourteen. Mary Machie's mother divorced. No one spoke about it. No one's parents got divorced then.

  In the same year Janet Wilson got pregnant. We listened in fascinated horror to her stories of secret unsuccessful visits to a back-street abortionist. One day she just wasn't at school. We heard she had been sent to live with an aunt until the baby was born and that her mother was going to bring up the baby as if it was hers. We never saw her again.

- The Abortion Act was passed in 1967. Abortion was legal if there was a threat to the mental or physical health of the mother, if the child was handicapped or born into bad conditions.

  In 1969 the law on divorce changed. Divorce was allowed if the marriage had broken down completely for two years. (Five years if one of the people did not agree.)

Protest

- With some friends I joined the Campaign for Nuclear Disarmament (CND). We wore badges and went to meetings. I wanted to go on the Easter march to Aldermaston, but my parents said no. I was furious. I went to a meeting in Trafalgar Square. It ended with a sit-down protest – and we were all taken away in police vans. Luckily I wasn't charged. In those days we believed we could change the world.

- The first British hydrogen bomb was tested in 1957. In 1963 there was a general ban on testing nuclear weapons above ground.

Question

Which do you think is best for finding out about post-war Britain – the personal memories or the historian's account? Explain why.

3.9 SOUTH AFRICA – A UNITED NATION?

South Africa today

Today people of all colours in South Africa are equal in the eyes of the law. But this was not so until 1994.

History of South Africa

Until the 1600s black native Africans lived in the area known as South Africa. Then the Dutch arrived. Soon they were followed by the British. The British pushed the Dutch further north and then finally conquered the whole area in 1902.

The white people in South Africa

White people made up only 15 per cent of all the people in South Africa. But white people controlled the country.

- Only white people could be elected to Parliament.
- All the best land was for white people (90 per cent of all the land).
- All the best jobs were for white people.
- Black people had to have passes to enter White areas.
- Black people had restricted rights at work.

South Africa.

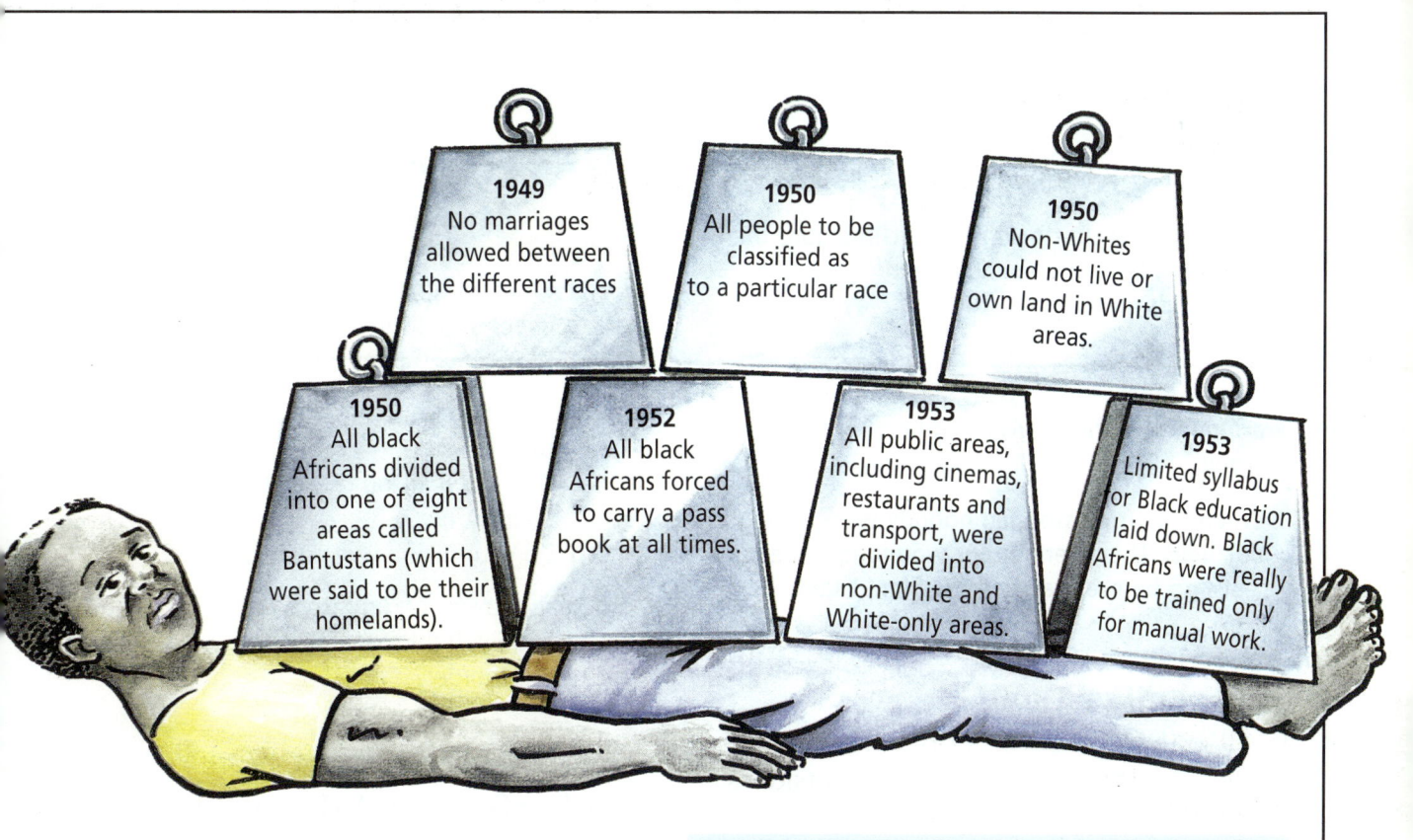

The establishment of apartheid, 1949–53.

Weights pressing down on a person:
- **1949** No marriages allowed between the different races
- **1950** All people to be classified as to a particular race
- **1950** Non-Whites could not live or own land in White areas.
- **1950** All black Africans divided into one of eight areas called Bantustans (which were said to be their homelands).
- **1952** All black Africans forced to carry a pass book at all times.
- **1953** All public areas, including cinemas, restaurants and transport, were divided into non-White and White-only areas.
- **1953** Limited syllabus for Black education laid down. Black Africans were really to be trained only for manual work.

The African National Congress (ANC)

Black Africans formed the ANC to work for equal rights in a peaceful way.

Apartheid, 1948

In 1948 the white Nationalist Party came to power. It passed a law setting up apartheid in South Africa. Apartheid means apart. Different races were to be kept apart, in different schools, in different towns, in different jobs, with different doctors, and so on.

The four races

The four different races in South Africa were:

- White
- Black
- Asian
- Coloured (mixed race).

Against apartheid

The non-white races of South Africa were furious about apartheid. In 1950 the ANC called a national strike. In 1954 a Freedom Charter was drawn up calling for the end of apartheid.

183

Source A

Written by a journalist at Sharpeville in 1960.

We heard the chatter of the machine gun, then another. There were people running towards me and I kept on taking pictures as I lay on the grass.

One of the policemen was standing on top of an armoured car firing his machine gun into the crowd.

When the firing stopped nobody was moving in our field. They were either wounded or dead. 'Let's go before they get our film,' I said.

Sharpeville, 1960

In 1960 thousands of people who were against apartheid demonstrated outside a police station at Sharpeville. The police panicked and 67 black Africans were shot dead. This made more people hate apartheid. The South African government was worried. It imprisoned about 12,000 people without a trial.

More arrests

The ANC gave up peaceful protest. More arrests followed. Three ANC leaders were imprisoned:

- Nelson Mandela
- Walter Sisulu
- Albert Luthuli.

They spent the next 26 years in prison. During the same time 69 other prisoners died under police interrogation.

Questions

1. Look at **Source A**.
   a. How were the people of Sharpeville killed?
   b. What was the journalist saying would happen to his film?
   c. Who do you think would do this and why?
2. Look at **Source B** and the section called **Sport**.
   a. Why did England cancel its cricket tour to South Africa?
   b. Do you think it was right to do so?
4. Read the section on **Steve Biko**. Why do you think the police were not blamed for his murder?

South Africa and the world

Many people, particularly in black countries, were horrified by what was going on in South Africa. In 1962 the United Nations set up a trade boycott (no countries were to trade with South Africa). But South Africa was such a wealthy country that other countries did not want to stop trading, so the boycott did not work.

Sport

In 1968, England's cricket team was going to play South Africa. One of the English team was a South African-born coloured person.

Source B

Headlines in the English newspaper, The Times, in September 1968.

- Vorster says MCC team unacceptable in South Africa
- D'Oliveira 'political cricket ball'
- Feeling of disgust over ban
- MCC call off tour of South Africa

Source C

A cartoon published in a South African newspaper in 1959. On the sign the writing is in English and Afrikaans.

The South Africans said he would not be welcome. England cancelled the cricket tour. Many other sports people refused to play in South Africa for years.

Apartheid under attack

Many people in South Africa demonstrated against apartheid. In 1976, 15,000 school pupils held a big demonstration against the government's policy that all school lessons must be in Afrikaans (the white language of South Africa).

Some changes, 1978

In 1978 P.W. Botha became President. He realised that apartheid could not go on if so many people in South Africa were against it. He wanted to win some of the Blacks over and so divide the opposition. He changed the law:

- Blacks could buy property in White areas.
- Blacks could join trade unions.
- Blacks could get a better education.
- Blacks did not have to carry pass books.
- Blacks and Whites could marry.

Did Botha's reforms work?

They did not work because Black Africans wanted proper equality and they went on fighting for it, led by people like Archbishop Desmond Tutu.

STEVE BIKO

Steve Biko was expelled from University for political activities. He helped found the Black Consciousness Movement in the 1960s. He was arrested several times and then finally in August 1977.

He was 30 years old and in good health. But in September 1977 he died of brain damage. The police said he had hit his head on the wall. All over the world people were outraged, but although there was an inquest, the police were not blamed.

Years later, at the Truth Commission, a police witness admitted that Biko died of being beaten.

More and more clashes

As time went on there were more and more clashes. There were disagreements between black groups. In some places law and order almost broke down completely. Botha declared a state of emergency again and there was more police brutality. Some foreign companies stopped trading with South Africa. Some people stopped buying food in supermarkets if it came from South Africa.

The end of apartheid

In 1989 F.W. de Klerk became President. He made moves towards ending apartheid.

- He lifted the ban on the ANC.
- He released Nelson Mandela from prison in 1990. (Mandela called off the ANC violence against the government.)

Record of Understanding

Talks were held during 1991 and 1992. The aim was to have equality in voting. It was very difficult. But an understanding was reached. De Klerk and Mandela were given the Nobel Peace Prize for their work. The first multiracial elections were held in April 1994.

The new multiracial government

The biggest vote went to the ANC (62 per cent). Nelson Mandela became President. De Klerk became Deputy President.

The new South African flag.

The Truth Commission

This was set up in 1996. Its aim was to uncover the truth so that South Africa could heal itself. Anyone coming forward to say what really happened would not be prosecuted.

People had mixed feelings about this. In 1984 the wife and daughter of Marius Schoon were blown up by a bomb planted by the security forces. At the Truth Commission, Craig Williamson admitted he had a part in the bombing. Marius said:

Suddenly their deaths are in the front of my mind again. Now it is personal. There is a good chance that I may actually shoot Williamson.

Source D

Nelson Mandela.

The future

As from 1994 apartheid was dead. South Africa was a multiracial society.

In 1995 black and white South Africans stood side by side to cheer their country to victory in the rugby World Cup.

However, there are still difficulties. There are many bitter memories. Also, at least two generations of black people do not have a good education, so it will take time for the country to build a future in which black people are fully involved.

Source E

An article in an English newspaper, 1998.

SECURITY POLICE PLOTTED MANDELA ASSASSINATION

An extraordinary story emerged after an informer admitted to the Truth Commission that he was hired for £31,000 to shoot Mr Mandela at his presidential ceremony in front of a world-wide television audience in 1994.

The informer had pulled out after he heard that security officers planned to shoot him immediately after the assassination and then claim the credit.

Detectives are investigating. They are said to have arrested a senior police officer and seized high-powered rifles.

Questions

1 Read the section on **The Truth Commission**.
   a When was it set up?
   b What is its aim?
   c Why do you think the Truth Commission said that people speaking the truth would not be prosecuted?
   d What has learning the truth done for Marius Schoon?

2 Read **Source E**.
   a Why did the informer decide not to shoot Mandela?
   b What do you think might have happened in South Africa if Mandela had been shot?
   c What do you think might happen to the informer now?
   d What can you learn about South Africa now from Source E?

GLOSSARY

Britain 1750–1900

abolitionists people who wanted slavery abolished, and who campaigned for this cause.

apprentices people (usually children) who learn a trade by working for a master for a certain period of time, for very low wages, and sometimes no wages at all, just food and lodgings.

benefit gain something good from.

blight a plant disease caused by fungus or insects.

Boston Tea Party an event of 1773 when Americans threw **cargoes** of tea into the water at Boston to protest against taxes imposed by the British government.

brimstone a historical word for sulphur, a yellow chemical element.

cargo goods carried by a ship, plane or vehicle.

cesspit an underground hole or container used for storing human waste.

drawbacks the difficulties or disadvantages of something.

enclosed when strip fields were done away with, and the land was turned into large fields with no strips, enclosed by fences and hedges.

estates groups in society, a bit like classes.

evict make someone leave their rented home, usually because of non-payment of rent.

fallow land that is left empty of crops for a while, to let it rest and improve before it is used again.

immigrants people who move to another country to live there permanently.

mania when something becomes so popular that people seem to be going mad about it.

oath of loyalty promising formally that you will remain faithful and loyal to something.

overseer someone whose job it is to watch to make sure work is being done properly.

petition a list of signatures from people protesting against something, used as a campaigning tool to show public opinion.

piles another word for haemorrhoids, swollen blood vessels at the opening of the anus.

registers books or papers used to record names, dates, events etc.

rotary motion round-and-round movement, like a wheel.

states smaller divisions of a country, making up a whole nation.

toll a fee paid to the owner of a road or bridge, to be able to travel on that land.

trade union an organisation of workers, set up to protect their rights and help each other.

transportation when criminals are sent to another country (usually a colony) instead of prison, as a punishment.

turnpike a road on which a **toll** had to be paid.

vaccinate to give someone a tiny amount of disease on purpose, so that their body can produce antibodies to fight the disease, making them immune to getting it again.

woolcombers people who combed wool using special tools, to make it ready for spinning.

worsted very fine wool cloth.

Twentieth Century World

abdicate stand down from power.

appeasement calm down an enemy by making concessions to them.

artillery large guns.

asylums mental hospitals.

black market illegal trade in hard-to-get goods (especially those on ration).

charismatic having charm which wins people over.

compensation money paid to make up for a loss, or a bad event.

conscientious because of your conscience – acting on something because your conscience tells you it is the right thing to do.

dictators people who rule alone with total authority.

dispatch rider a motorcycle courier.

inflation when prices go up, but money is not worth more.

Kaiser the title of the king of Germany.

malaria a disease in hot countries, carried by mosquitoes and passed on to people and animals when the mosquito bites them.

oilfields areas of land under which there is oil.

Quaker a member of the religious group, the Society of Friends, founded in 1668. Quakers are pacifists.

radiation energy given out by radioactive things, which can harm people.

reconnaissance going near an enemy to try and find out details about it or the land it is on.

recruits very new members of the armed forces.

rivals enemies or opposing teams in competition against each other.

sanctions the stopping of trade between one country and another country as punishment.

sonar a system whereby objects can be detected even when they are far away, by bouncing sound waves off them.

tribunals boards set up to judge over matters of public concern.

INDEX

Africa 12, 167, 176
   South Africa 10, 182–7
   Southern Africa 9
African National Congress 182, 183, 184, 186, 187
agriculture 26–7, 31, 32–3, 39
   crop rotation 32
   enclosures 33
   livestock 33
   machinery 33, 89, 95
   strip farming 32
America 6, 12, 22, 33, 78–9 (*see also* United States of America)
   American Civil War 79
   independence 72, 75
Amritsar Massacre 168–9
apartheid 183–5, 186
Arkwright, Richard 44
Australia 6, 10, 11, 22–3, 102
Austria:
   and Napoleon 86
   First World War 102, 118, 119
   Second World War 127

battles:
   Trafalgar 86
   Waterloo 87
Belgium 102, 128
Berlin Wall 151, 162, 163
Biko, Steve 185
black people 12, 156, 182–6
   in Britain 13, 16–17
Bolsheviks 120
Boston Massacre 74
Boston Tea Party 75
Botha, PW 185–6
Boulton, Matthew 37
Bridgewater, Duke of 63
buffer states 151, 162
Bulgaria 118, 162

Campaign for Nuclear Disarmament 181
Canada 9, 11, 102
capitalism 100, 162–3
Cartwright, Edmund 44
census 38
Ceylon (*see* Sri Lanka)
Chartists 92–3
children 39, 45, 48, 55, 56–7, 58–9, 70, 94–5, 97, 125, 136–7
China 101, 126, 162, 171

Clarkson, Thomas 14
Clive, Robert 19
communications 20, 101
communism 100, 101, 121, 151, 162–3, 170
Cook, James 10
Cuba 163, 164–5
Czechoslovakia 119, 127, 162

Davy, Humphrey 59
de Klerk, FW 186, 187
Denmark 128
disease 27, 39, 42–3, 101
   cholera 42–3, 46–7, 69
   smallpox 39, 101, 175
domino theory 162, 170

East India Company 18
education 68, 95, 97, 167, 180
empires 6, 7, 98, 166–7
   British 6, 8–11, 72, 74–5, 166–9, 182
   French 86–7, 166–7, 170
   German 119
   Italian 121
   Japanese 131, 152–3
   Napoleon 86–7
   Spanish 166

factories 4, 13, 30–1, 39, 44–5, 48–9, 54–5, 69
fascism 121
Festival of Britain 178
First World War 100, 102–11, 116–17, 118–19
   conscientious objectors 108–9
   conscription 108
   deserters 110–11
   mutineers 110–11
   Treaty of Versailles 118–19, 126
   trench warfare 104–7
   Western Front 103, 104, 110
   women 116–17
France 18, 19, 122, 123
   and America 74, 75, 79
   First World War 102, 118–19
   French Revolution 72, 80–3
   Napoleon 81, 84–7
   Second World War 127, 128, 140, 142, 150
   Vichy government 128, 145

Gandhi, Mahatma 19, 166, 167

Germany:
   Division 150–1, 162
   First World War 102, 118–19
   post–First World War 122–7
   Second World War 127–30, 132–5, 140–1, 144, 147, 150–1, 156–61
Goebbels, Joseph 125

health 6, 39, 101, 178
Hitler 122, 123–7, 130, 132, 140, 150
Holland (*see* Netherlands)
Hong Kong 9
housing 40, 52, 178
Hungary 102, 118, 119, 162, 163

India 9, 10, 18–19, 167, 168–9
industry (*see also* factories; mining; revolutions, industrial)
   cotton 44, 54–5, 56
   domestic system 30, 44, 48
   factory system 44
   machinery 30, 44, 49, 50, 54, 88–9
   wool 4, 30, 44, 48–9, 50–1
inventors 36–7, 44, 49, 59, 64
Ireland 26–9
Iron Curtain 151
Italy 102, 121, 126

Japan 126, 131, 152–5
Jews 46, 125, 141, 156–61

land ownership 26, 32–3
League of Nations 126, 174
leisure 52–3, 71
Lenin 120–1
Lord Haw–Haw 145
Luddites 88–9

Malaya 152–3
Mandela, Nelson 184, 186, 187
Maquis 140
McAdam, John 62
migration 6, 10, 11–15, 22–3, 28, 49, 79
mining 30, 58–61, 64
mining villages 60
Mussolini 121
My Lai Massacre 172–3

Napoleon 9, 72, 81, 84–7
nationalism 167

NATO 163
Nazi Party 123–5
Nelson, Lord 86
Netherlands (Holland) 128, 141, 182
New Zealand 6, 10, 11, 33, 102
Newcomen, Thomas 36
Norway 128, 144

P&O 20, 21
Pankhurst family 112, 113, 116
People's Charter 92
Pétain, Henri Philippe 145
Poland 127, 128, 156–7, 162
population 6, 26, 30, 32, 33, 38–9
ports 4, 11, 14

Quisling, Vidkun 144

Rasputin 120
Rebecca Riots 90–1
Revere, Paul 76–7
revolutions:
    agricultural 32–3
    American 72, 74–7
    and Britain 73, 88–93
    French 7, 72, 80–3
    industrial 30–1, 36–7
    Russian 120–1
Robespierre 80
Romania 162
Russia (see also Soviet Union)
    and Napoleon 87
    First World War 102, 118
    revolution 120–1
    Second World War 130

Salt, Titus 50–3
Saltaire 52–3
Sassoon, Siegfried 110
Savery, Thomas 36
Second World War 100, 127–61,
    166–7, 174
    at sea 129, 153
    Battle of Britain 132
    Blitz 132–4, 138, 139
    Britain 127, 128, 129, 132–4, 135,
    136–9, 142–3, 147–9, 150, 153,
    178–9
    camps (concentration, labour,
    death) 156, 158–60
    collaborators 144–5
    D-Day 150
    Dresden 135

Dunkirk 128
Enigma machine 147
evacuation 136–7
ghettos 156–8
Hiroshima 154–5
Holocaust 156–61
Home Guard 179
Local Defence Volunteers 179
Nagasaki 154
Operation Barbarossa 130
Operation Sealion 132
Pearl Harbor 131, 148, 152, 153
rationing 138, 139, 148, 179
resistance 140–3
secret agents 142–3
Special Operations Executive
    142–3
spying 129, 142–3, 146–7
traitors 144–5
Serbia 102
Sharpeville 183, 184
Singapore 10, 152
slavery 11–17, 79
Soviet Union (USSR) 121, 171
    Cold War 162–5
    Second World War 150, 151
Sri Lanka (Ceylon) 9, 167
St Peter's Fields 73
Stalin 121
Statue of Liberty 78, 79
steam power 30, 36–7, 44, 64
Stephenson, George 64
Stresemann, Gustav 123
suffragettes 112–17
Swing Riots 89

Telford, Thomas 62
Tolpuddle Martyrs 22, 24–5, 73
town life 4, 30, 31, 39, 40–5, 46, 48,
    50, 52–3, 96–7
towns 31, 39, 48, 50, 52–3
trade 4, 6, 8, 10–15, 18, 74
    slave 11–15
trade unions 7, 24, 88
transport 4, 13, 31, 62–7
    canals 31, 63
    railways 31, 64–7, 68
    roads 31, 62
    sea 20, 21
transportation 22–5
Trevithick, Richard 64
Trotsky 121

Truth Commission 186
Tsar Nicholas II 120
Turkey 118, 119
turnpike roads 62, 90–1
Tutu, Archbishop Desmond 185

United Nations 174–7, 184
United States of America 75, 99,
    118–19, 123
    Cold War 162–5
    Second World War 131, 135,
    148–9, 150, 152–5
    Vietnam 170–3
USSR (see Soviet Union)

village life 4, 24, 30, 32–5, 39, 94–5
voting rights 7, 88, 92, 112–17

war 7, 9, 10, 100
    guerrilla warfare 171
    weapons 105, 132–5, 154, 171,
    181
wars (see also First World War;
    Second World War)
    American Civil War 79
    American War of Independence
    75–6
    British-French war in America 74
    British-French war in India 18–19
    Cold War 100, 151, 162–5
    Gulf War 177
    Korean War 163, 176
    Napoleonic wars 86–7
    Vietnam War 163, 170–3
Warsaw Pact 163
Watt, James 36–7
Wedgwood, Josiah 63
Weimar Republic 122–3
Wellington, Duke of 87
West Indies 12
Wilberforce, William 14
women 7, 48, 68–9, 70, 94–7,
    112–17, 138–9, 180, 181
work 4, 28
    domestic service 16, 70–1, 95, 96
    farming 24, 30, 94, 95
    in factories 44–5, 52–3, 56
    in offices 71
    in towns 96–7
    mining 58–61

Yugoslavia 119, 162

Heinemann Educational
Halley Court, Jordan Hill, Oxford OX2 8EJ
a division of Reed Educational and Professional
Publishing Ltd

OXFORD MELBOURNE AUCKLAND
JOHANNESBURG BLANTYRE GABORONE
IBADAN PORTSMOUTH (NH) USA CHICAGO

Heinemann is a registered trademark of
Reed Educational and Professional Publishing Ltd

© Fiona Reynoldson and David Taylor 1998

The right of Fiona Reynoldson and David Taylor to be identified as the authors of this work has been asserted by them in accordance with Copyright, Designs and Patent Act.

ISBN 0 435 30964 1

02 01 00
10 9 8 7 6 5 4 3

British Library cataloguing in Publication data for this title is available from the British Library.

Printed and bound in Spain by Edelvives, Zaragoza

Illustrations by Sally Artz, Stephen Wisdom and Visual Image.

Photographic acknowledgements

The authors and publisher would like to thank the following for permission to reproduce photographs:

Cover photograph: Bridgeman/Manchester City Art Library, Imperial War Museum

Britain 1750-1900

AKG: 3.5D
Birmingham City Library: p5D
Bradford Libraries: 2.8A, C, 2.9A, B, C, D
Bridgeman: 1.1A, 1.2G, 2.13F, 2.14D, 3.4B, 3.5B,
British Museum: p4A
Cfarthfa Castle: 2.14A, B
Catherine Emmerson: 3.9A
e.t. Archive: 1.1C, 2.1D, 2.2A
Fotomas: 1.6B, 2.5M
Getty Images: 1.4B
Giraudon: 3.3A
Chris Honeywell: 2.5E

Hulton Getty: 1.5B
J. Meakin: 2.3D
Katz: 2.1C, 2.7A
Lancaster City Museums: 1.2D
Mary Evans: p7F, 1.6C, 1.7B, 2.5A, C, D, 2.11A, 2.12F, 2.13A,
Michael Holford: 1.4A
Museum of English Rural Life: 3.9C
National Library of Wales: 3.7B, D
National Portrait Gallery: 1.1B
National Trust: p4B
Paul Revere Memorial Association: 3.2C
PRO: 3.6D
Punch: 2.5H, 3.6C
Quarry Bank Mill: 2.10A, B, C, 2.11B, C
Salvation Army: p6E
Sotheby's: 1.2H
The Science Museum: 2.1A
Thomas Nelson: 1.3A
Topham: 2.1B
Wansdworth Library: p5C
West Sussex Record Office: 2.14C

Twentieth Century World

AKG: 2.1A, C, 2.4D
Punch/Centre for the Study of Cartoons: 2.4A
Bridgeman: 1.2B
Corbis: 2.11D
e.t. Archive: 1.3E, 2.13H
Getty: 2.5A, F
Hulton Getty: 1.4B, 2.1B, 2.3D
Imperial War Museum: 1.2C, E, 1.3C, 1.4H, 2.3B, 2.8A, C, p143, 2.11A, 2.12B, 2.14F
Katherine Jenerette: 3.6C
Katz: 3.4D
Kobal Collection: 3.3B
Liddle Collection/University of Leeds: 1.3B
David Low/Centre for the Study of Cartoons: 3.5C, 3.6A
Magnum: 2.9A
Mary Evans: 1.3A, 1.4A, C, 2.10B
Mirror Syndication: 2.10C
Museum of London: 1.4G
Nationalmuseet Denmark: 2.7B
Popperfoto: 2.10A, 2.11E, 2.14A, 3.3A
SCR: 2.7D
Topham: 2.14E
Yad Vashem: 2.14B

The publishers have made every effort to trace copyright holders of material in this book. Any